99 CASSEROLE DISHES

MARI LAJOS — KÁROLY HEMZŐ

with 33 COLOUR PHOTOGRAPHS

Corvina

Original title: 99 egytálétel 33 színes fotóval
Corvina Kiadó, Budapest, 1988

Translated by Judith Elliott
Consultant: J. Audrey Ellison
Design by Vera Köböl
©Mari Lajos and Károly Hemző

Recipes compiled under the professional supervision of Gyula
Gullner, execûtive chef at the Hotel Duna·Intercontinental,
Budapest

On the cover: Stuffed peppers

ISBN 963 13 2774 4
CO 2718-h-8991
Printed in Hungary, 1989
Athenaeum Printing House, Budapest

PREFACE

Casseroles were the fare of peoples who lived close to nature and had to accommodate their daily lives to the vagaries of the weather. Some of these dishes were rich in variety, some were meagre, due, perhaps, to a shortage of ingredients or preparation time.

In today's rushed and hectic world, why should we always expect the homemaker to have plenty of time, especially when there are so many other things to do? I am convinced that in spite of the problems of shopping and the lack of time, there are many of us who like to bring pleasure to the rest of the family and think it important that our overburdened children and harassed partners should be drawn to the table by delicious aromas to enjoy good food and pleasant conversation.

With some exaggeration I could suggest that you empty your shopping basket, see what your refrigerator or larder contains, bring out your spices and concoct some interesting combination, then, using a pressure cooker, a frying pan or a fireproof dish, produce a really delicious meal in a matter of minutes. Make sure, however, that it not only *tastes* good but also *looks* good and, furthermore, that it is nutritious. After all, only one dish will be set on the table.

However, the task is not as simple as it sounds. You still have to plan a casserole dish to a certain extent, although less time will be needed than when cooking items separately. In fact, new creations can be concocted using leftovers.

A peculiarity of the casserole is that it is named after the ingredient that happens to be predominant. But despite the many variations, there is one thing which all casseroles have in common. The ingredients of the dish are cooked together, and the ensuing combination of flavours and aromas gives it its unique character.

In this volume, the dishes are grouped according to the season in which the various vegetables are readily available. But this is only in principle, since deep-frozen vegetables can be obtained all year round.

Note : Unless otherwise stated, the quantities in the recipes are sufficient for four portions.

In this series all weights and liquid measures are given in metric and Imperial. It is essential that *either* the metric *or* the Imperial measurements should be used, as the quantities vary slightly, and mixing the two could result in the wrong proportions.

VEGETABLE DISHES

Spinach-and-potato bake

700 g	spinach or chard	1½ lb
500 g	spicy cooking sausage	1¼ lb
400 g	potatoes	1 lb
200 g	uncooked smoked ham	7 oz
100 g	smoked bacon	4 oz
2	eggs	2
1	sprig fresh rosemary	1
8–10	fresh basil leaves	8–10
1	clove garlic	1
1 tsp	dried marjoram	1 tsp
3 tbs	brandy	3 tbs
	nutmeg	
	salt	
	pepper	
1–2 tbs	oil	1–2 tbs
1	medium onion	1

Wash the spinach in plenty of water, drain well, put in a pan with a little salt, cover with a lid and cook over a moderate heat. When tender squeeze out the excess liquid.

Remove the skin from the sausage, slice and put in a pan. Add the finely chopped onion, rosemary and basil, the crushed garlic, the marjoram and a pinch of nutmeg. Season to taste with salt and pepper. Fry over a high heat for a few minutes, adding a drop of oil if necessary. Leave to cool, then stir in the egg and brandy.

Line a fireproof dish with the bacon cut into very thin slices. Spoon half the sausage mixture over the bacon. Then add a layer of sliced ham, followed by half the spinach. Add another layer of the sausage, ham and spinach.

Peel and wash the potatoes. Dry on kitchen paper, cut into thin slices and arrange in a circle round the edge of the dish. Sprinkle with salt, pour over the oil and bake in a moderate oven (180° C/350° F/Gas 4) for 1–1½ hours until the potato is golden brown. Serve at once.

Spinach, curd cheese and mushroom strudel

1 kg	spinach	2¼ lb
300 g	curd cheese	11 oz
1	egg	1
1	egg yolk	1
100 g	button mushrooms	4 oz
1	clove garlic	1
400 g	deep frozen puff pastry	14 oz
50 g	grated cheese	2 oz
	salt, pepper	
	nutmeg	
	breadcrumbs	

Wash the spinach carefully in plenty of water. Drain, then place in a pan with a little salt. Cover and cook over a moderate heat until tender. Squeeze out any excess liquid. Chop and place in a deep bowl. Add the curd cheese, the whole egg, the grated cheese, crushed garlic and a pinch of nutmeg. Season to taste with salt and pepper. Beat well until smooth. Finally add the washed, dried and finely chopped mushrooms.

Roll out the pastry until very thin on a clean, floured tea towel. Sprinkle with breadcrumbs then spread the spinach mixture evenly over the pastry. Add another sprinkling of breadcrumbs, and with the help of the tea towel lightly roll up the pastry. Turn under the two ends so that the filling does not escape during baking. Place on a greased baking tray and prick the top with a fork. Brush with the beaten egg yolk and bake in a hot oven (200° C/400° F/Gas 5) until golden brown for about 30 minutes.

Allow to cool until just warm before slicing. This dish is also delicious served cold.

Spinach ring

1 kg	spinach	2¼ lb
4	eggs	4
1	clove garlic	1
100 ml	milk	4 fl oz
100 g	grated cheddar cheese	4 oz
80 g	butter	3 oz
	salt, pepper	
	breadcrumbs	
150 g	thin spaghetti	5 oz

Spinach ring

4

400 ml	tomato sauce (see p. 61)	14 fl oz
100–150 g	grated parmesan cheese	4–5 oz

Wash the spinach thoroughly in plenty of water. Drain, then cut into finger-width strips. Heat half the butter in a pan, then add the milk, the spinach and crushed garlic. Season with salt and pepper. Cover with a lid and cook over a moderate heat until the spinach is nearly done. Then remove the lid and continue cooking until the liquid has evaporated. Put aside to cool. Mix in the grated cheese and the eggs and beat together with a little salt. Butter a ring tin and sprinkle with breadcrumbs. Spoon in the spinach mixture. Press the cooked spaghetti into the spinach. Melt the remaining butter and pour over the top. Bake in a moderate oven (180° C/350° F/Gas 4) for 25–30 minutes or until golden brown. Remove from the oven and leave for a few minutes before carefully turning out onto a hot serving dish.

Serve immediately with grated cheese and hot tomato sauce in a sauce boat.

Chard-and-cheese bake

1 kg	chard	2½ lb
2	medium onions	2
80 g	lean, smoked sausage	3 oz
4	medium firm tomatoes	4
250 g	cheese (emmenthal, edam, trappist)	½ lb
250 g	cooked ham	½ lb
200 g	cooked rice	7 oz
2	eggs	2
	nutmeg, salt, pepper	
1	knob butter	1

Wash the chard and drain in a colander. Remove any of the thick stems and chop. Cut the leaves into finger-width pieces. (The stems are very good to eat and have a flavour quite similar to asparagus.)

Put the chard into a pan of boiling, slightly salted water and cook for 5 minutes. Drain and leave to cool slightly before squeezing out any liquid.

Dice the bacon into a pan and fry, then add the finely chopped onion. Cover and cook gently until the onion is transparent. Peel the tomatoes (see p. 62). Grate the cheese and dice the ham.

Butter a fireproof dish. Place the rice at the bottom, followed by the chard, the onion, the ham and the tomatoes cut into thin segments. Sprinkle ⅔ of the cheese on top. Season to taste with salt,

pepper and nutmeg. Beat the eggs slightly, add the remaining cheese and pour over the top. Bake in a hot oven (220° C/425° F/Gas 6) for 15–20 minutes or until golden brown.

Note! Serve immediately, otherwise the cheese will harden.

Carrot and spinach flan

for the pastry		
300 g	plain flour	11 oz
200 g	butter or margarine	7 oz
	salt	
for the filling		
500 g	spinach	1¼ lb
500 g	young carrots	1¼ lb
80 g	butter	3 oz
50 g	blanched and lightly roasted almonds	2 oz
100 g	grated cheese	4 oz
1	large bunch parsley	1
	salt, pepper	
1	egg yolk for brushing	1

Prepare puff pastry with the flour, butter and a little water. Shape into a ball and put in a cold place for 1 hour. Then roll out onto a floured surface. Line a buttered and floured loose-bottomed flan tin with the pastry. Trim the edges and set the trimmings aside for decoration.

Wash the spinach thoroughly in plenty of water. Drain and chop, then place in a pan with a little salt and cook gently until tender. When cool, squeeze out any excess liquid. Return it to the pan and toss in a little hot butter.

Scrape and slice the carrots. Place in a pan with a knob of butter, a little salt and the chopped parsley. Cover and simmer until tender.

Place a layer of spinach into the flan tin. Add a sprinkling of roast, chopped almonds, grated cheese and pepper, followed by a layer of carrots. Continue adding the layers, finishing with spinach topped with chopped almonds and grated cheese. Pour the remaining melted butter on top.

Roll out the remaining pastry. Using a fluted pastry wheel, cut into narrow strips ½ cm (¼ in) wide. Lay these in a lattice pattern on top of the filling. Brush with beaten egg yolk and bake in a moderate oven (180° C/350° F/Gas 4) for 30–35 minutes until golden brown. Ease out of the tin, place on a hot serving plate and serve at once, cut into wedges.

Note! This dish is also excellent served cold.

Asparagus paté

500 g	asparagus	1¼ lb
3	young carrots	3
250 g	cooked ham	½ lb
250 g	cooked, spicy sausage	½ lb
1	dry roll	1
100 ml	milk	4 fl oz
2	eggs	2
½ tsp	sugar	½ tsp
	salt	
	nutmeg	
5–6	vine leaves	5–6
1	knob butter	1

Cut off the woody parts from the base of the asparagus stems and scrape the white parts using a sharp knife, then tie into a bundle. Wash and scrape the carrots. Bring water to the boil in two pans, add a little salt and sugar and cook or preferably steam the asparagus and carrots until tender. Drain thoroughly in a colander.

Slice the ham, remove the skin from the sausage and soak the roll in the milk. Then put through a mincer two or three times to get a smooth paste. Mix in the beaten eggs, nutmeg and salt to taste. Blend well together until creamy.

Wash the vine leaves in several lots of water. Blanch in slightly salted water then drain in a colander.

Butter a terrine or fireproof dish and line with half of the vine leaves. Spread half the sausage mixture on top. Then arrange half of the asparagus on the sausage, followed by all the carrots. Add the remaining asparagus and cover with the other half of the sausage mixture. Cover with the vine leaves and dot with butter.

Cover with kitchen foil and stand in tepid water in a deep baking tray.

Bake in a moderate oven (180° C/350° F/Gas 4) for approximately 1 hour. Leave to cool, then turn out onto an oblong dish. If it does not come out easily, stand the terrine in boiling water for 1 or 2 minutes.

Cut into fingers and decorate the top with slices of hard boiled egg or tomatoes. Serve with toast.

Carrot and spinach flan

Stuffed kohlrabi with mushrooms

8	young kohlrabi	8
1	medium onion	1
1 tbs	oil	1 tbs
150 g	button mushrooms	5 oz
150 g	cooked ham	5 oz
1	pinch marjoram	1
1	small bunch parsley	1
1	egg	1
150 ml	meat stock (made from a cube)	¼ pt
	salt	
	pepper	
1	knob butter	1

Peel the kohlrabi and cook for 15 minutes in slightly salted boiling water. Drain, then cut out the middle, leaving a thickness of about 1 cm (½ in) all round.

Dice the middle parts of the kohlrabi. Fry the finely chopped onion in the oil until transparent, then add the diced mushroom.

Season with salt and pepper, cover and simmer until tender. Put aside to cool, then add the diced ham, the chopped parsley, the marjoram and more pepper to taste. Finally add the diced kohlrabi and egg. Blend well together.

Stuff the kohlrabi and arrange in a deep baking tray. Pour in the meat stock, cover with kitchen foil and bake in a moderate oven (180° C/350° F/ Gas 4) for 20 minutes. Remove the foil, pour the melted butter over the kohlrabi and return to the oven for another 15 minutes or until light golden brown.

Stuffed kohlrabi for spring

8	young kohlrabi with leaves	8
400 g	minced pork	1 lb
80 g	cooked rice	3 oz
1	egg	1
1	large bunch parsley	1
	salt	
	pepper	
30 g	butter	1 oz

Stuffed kohlrabi for spring

40 g	flour	1½ oz
200 ml	double cream or soured cream	7 fl oz
500 ml	meat stock (made from a cube)	1 pt

This dish is really at its best in spring, when the kohlrabi is still very young.

Peel the kohlrabi and cut out the middle from the root side. Put one or two of the large outer leaves aside to use like vine leaves for any extra stuffing. Wash the young inner leaves and cut into narrow strips. Blend the meat, egg and chopped parsley together, then season to taste with salt. Add a generous amount of pepper, followed by the rice. Stuff the kohlrabi and wrap any extra stuffing in the leaves.

Place the middle parts of the kohlrabi in a large pan, then arrange the stuffed kohlrabi and the leaves on top. Lay the chopped leaves between the kohlrabi, pour in the meat stock and bring to the boil. Cover and simmer until tender.

Using a perforated spoon, carefully lift out the stuffed kohlrabi and the stuffed leaves. Make a roux and with the addition of some water and double or soured cream, bring to the boil. Return the kohlrabi to the meat stock and bring to the boil once again.

Serve sprinkled with chopped parsley.

Chicken and kohlrabi

4	chicken breasts or legs	4
1 kg	young kohlrabi	2¼ lb
3 tbs	oil	3 tbs
40 g	plain flour	1½ oz
200–300 ml	soured cream	7–10 fl oz
1	bunch parsley	1
3	cloves garlic	3
½ tsp	paprika	½ tsp
	salt	
	pepper	

Wash and dry the chicken. Cut each piece in half. Flash fry until slightly browned, then remove from the pan and put aside. Pour the oil into a large pan. Place a layer of peeled, finger-length strips of kohlrabi in the bottom of the pan. Arrange the chicken on top. Season to taste with salt and pepper. Add the crushed garlic and cover with the remaining kohlrabi. Pour on a little water, cover and cook over a moderate heat until tender, shaking the pan gently from time to time.

Make a roux with the rest of the oil and the flour. Remove from the heat, add the paprika and 200 ml (7 fl oz) water. Stir until smooth. Remove the chicken pieces from the pan before pouring in the sauce. Add the soured cream and bring to the boil, stirring until thick. Return the chicken to the pan, sprinkle with chopped parsley and serve immediately.

Note! Use fresh, young kohlrabi only.

Greek chicken with kohlrabi

6	young kohlrabi	6
30 g	butter	1 oz
1	bunch parsley	1
4 (800 g)	boned chicken breasts	4 (1¾ lb)
200 g	feta cheese	7 oz
12–16	green or black olives	12–16
½ tsp	paprika	½ tsp
	salt	
	pepper	
	flour	
	oil	

Peel and wash the kohlrabi, then cut into finger-sized strips. Place in a pan with the butter, and salt and pepper to taste. Cover and cook over a moderate heat until tender. Add a little water if necessary. Remove from the heat and keep warm. Beat the chicken breast slices gently with a meat mallet. Sprinkle with salt and put aside for 30 minutes. Turn in flour seasoned with the paprika, then fry in a little oil until golden brown on both sides. Lay a thin slice of cheese on each piece of chicken, cover with a lid for a few minutes, just enough to allow the cheese to melt. Arrange on a hot serving dish. Sprinkle with the stoned, halved olives and arrange the kohlrabi round the edge. Finally, add the chopped parsley and serve at once.

Note! Use young kohlrabi only. Take care when adding salt, as the cheese and olives are quite salty.

Layered pork chops with cauliflower

8	slices pork chops or shank	8
8	thin slices cooked daisy ham	8
8	thin slices of soft cheese	8

Layered pork chops with cauliflower

1 kg	cauliflower, cleaned	2¼ lb
600 ml	soured cream	1 pt
3	egg yolks	3
50 g	grated cheese	2 oz
1	bunch parsley	1
	mustard	
	flour	
	oil	
	breadcrumbs	
	salt	
	pepper	

Wash and gently pound the meat. Salt and let stand for 30 minutes, then turn into flour to which some ground pepper has been added. Precook for a few minutes on both sides in hot oil, then set aside. Wash the cauliflower and cook until tender in slightly salted water. Let drip, then carefully separate the florets.

Butter a deep baking dish and sprinkle with breadcrumbs. Place one layer of cauliflower on the bottom. Spread a thin layer of mustard on the meat, add a slice of cheese, a slice of ham, and place on top of the cauliflower. Spread the rest of the cauliflower on top, sprinkle with egg yolks, the grated cheese, the chopped parsley, and the soured cream salted to taste. Bake in a hot (200° C/ 400° F/ Gas 6-7) preheated oven for 20-25 minutes. Serve immediately.

Mexican stuffed cymling

8	small cymling	8
400 g	Mexican mixed vegetables (100 g – 4 oz green peas, the same amount of corn, carrots, and cut string beans)	1 lb
200 g	chicken liver	7 oz
200 ml	Béchamel sauce (p. 61)	7 fl oz
1	egg yolk	1
80 g	grated cheese	3 oz
	salt, pepper, breadcrumbs	
	ground nutmeg	
	pat of butter	
1 tbsp	oil	1 tbsp
4-5	sage leafs	4-5
1	bunch parsley	1

Wash the cymling and scoop out the inside, leaving only a 1 cm (½ in) thick wall. Salt, turn upside down and let stand for 30 minutes. Wash and cut the chicken liver into cubes and cook for 5-8 minutes in hot oil with the crumbled sage leafs and ground black pepper. In the meantime, cook the vegetable mix in a little lightly salted water until tender, and drain. Make the Béchamel sauce. Slowly mix with the vegetables, chicken liver, chopped parsley, 50 g (2 oz) of the grated cheese, and stuff the cymlings with this mixture. Place the cymlings side by side in a buttered baking dish sprinkled with breadcrumbs, and sprinkle the top with the remaining cheese. Cover with aluminum foil and bake in a moderate oven (180° C/ 350° F/Gas 4) for 25 minutes. Remove the foil and continue to bake for an additional 15-20 minutes. *Note!* This dish can also be made with young vegetable marrow or large-size courgettes.

Mexican stuffed cymling

Carrot-and-ham soufflé with peas

1 kg	carrots	2¼ lb
150 g	onion	5 oz
200 g	cooked ham	7 oz
150 g	peas (fresh or deep-frozen)	5 oz
6	eggs	6
100 ml	milk	4 fl oz
500 ml	chicken stock (made from a cube)	1 pt
	nutmeg	
	salt	
	pepper	
1	knob butter	1
	parsley	

Scrape the carrots and cut into strips 5 cm (2 in) long and ½ cm (¼ in) thick. Slice the onion and put aside 8 large rings. Place the carrots and onions in a pan, add a little boiling chicken stock, season with salt and pepper, cover and cook over a moderate heat until tender. Drain thoroughly in a colander and leave to cool. Cut the ham into thin strips.

Beat the eggs with the milk, nutmeg and a little salt and pepper in a bowl. Stir in the cooked vegetables and the ham then pour into a buttered fireproof dish. Arrange the onion rings round the edge of the dish. Place in a hot oven (200° C/400° F/ Gas 6) and bake for 30 minutes. (Do not open the oven door, otherwise the soufflé will flop.)

Meanwhile, cook the peas in the remaining chicken stock until tender, then drain well. When the soufflé is cooked, arrange a little pile of peas in the centre of each onion ring.

Serve at once, sprinkled with a little chopped parsley.

Tenderloin hotpot with peas

400 g	pork fillet or tenderloin	1 lb
1	large onion	1
2	cloves garlic	2
	fat	
50 g	smoked fat bacon	2 oz
	marjoram	
	salt	

	pepper	
	paprika	
600 g	peas (fresh or deep-frozen)	1¼ lb
1	large bunch parsley	1

Wash and dry the meat, then cut into strips approximately 5 cm (2 in) long and 3 cm (1½ in) thick. Slice the bacon into very thin strips and fry. Add the sliced onion (separated into rings) and the thinly sliced garlic to the bacon. Cover and fry over a moderate heat until transparent. Add the meat, season to taste with salt and paprika. Sprinkle generously with freshly ground pepper and add the chopped marjoram. Fry for a few minutes over a high heat to brown the meat, then cover and simmer until tender. Remove the lid, turn up the hat and cook until the liquid has reduced, and is no longer runny.

Meanwhile, cook the peas in a little salted water. Drain them in a colander and add to the meat, stirring gently. Heat for a minute or two, then spoon into a hot deep serving dish.

Sprinkle the top with chopped parsley and serve at once.

Italian-style broccoli and kidney bake

(for 4–5 people)

4	pig's kidneys	4
400 g	pork tenderloin	1 lb
1	large onion	1
2	cloves garlic	2
3 tbs	oil	3 tbs
1	young kohlrabi	1
2 tbs	wine vinegar	2 tbs
500 g	broccoli	1¼ lb
500 g	potatoes	1¼ lb
1	sprig fresh basil	1
1	knob butter	1
100 ml	dry white wine	4 fl oz
100 ml	meat stock (from a cube)	4 fl oz
	salt	
	pepper	

Wash the kidneys, halve and cut out the core. Lay in a flat dish, sprinkle with the vinegar and add enough cold water to cover. Put aside for 1 hour,

Italian-style broccoli and kidney bake

then rinse under running water, drain and cut into thin strips. Wash and dry the pork, then cut into 2 cm (¾ in) cubes. Dice the onion and garlic and fry in the oil until transparent. Add the kidney and meat and fry over a high heat for a few minutes. Peel the kohlrabi and cut into thin strips. Peel and slice the potatoes. Wash the broccoli, drain well and divide into florets. Chop the basil finely. Butter an ovenproof dish. Using half the vegetables arrange them in layers, starting with the potatoes, then the broccoli and finally the kohlrabi. Season with salt and pepper and a sprinkling of basil. Lay the meat evenly on top, followed by the remaining potatoes, broccoli and kohlrabi. Season with salt, pepper and basil. Pour in the wine and meat stock and bake in a hot oven (220° C/425° F/Gas 7) for about 1 hour until the vegetables are tender. Serve at once.

Layered French-bean bake à la Theresa

1 kg	French or runner beans (fresh or deep-frozen)	2¼ lb
250 g	smoked, boned belly of pork	½ lb
200 g	smoked cheese	7 oz
30 g	tomato purée	1 oz
200 ml	soured cream	7 fl oz
1	knob butter	1
8	eggs	8
	salt	
	breadcrumbs	
	parsley	

Prepare the French beans and cook until tender in lightly salted boiling water. Drain in a colander. Butter a large fireproof dish and sprinkle with breadcrumbs. Arrange a layer of beans at the bottom of the dish, followed by some of the diced pork. Then sprinkle with a little of the grated cheese. Continue alternating between beans, meat and cheese until all the ingredients have been used up. Finish with a layer of green beans. Mix the soured cream and tomato purée together, add a little salt and then pour evenly over the beans. Then using a small ladle make eight wells or nests in the top (big enough for an egg to go in). Bake in a moderate oven (180° C/350° F/Gas 4) for 30 minutes till the top is golden brown. Remove from the oven and slip an egg into each nest. Return to the oven and bake until the egg whites have solidified. Sprinkle the top with chopped parsley and serve at once.

Ham and cauliflower au gratin

1 kg	cauliflower (fresh or deep-frozen)	2¼ lb
150 ml	meat stock (made with a cube)	¼ pt
1 tbs	lemon juice	1 tbs
150 g	uncooked smoked sliced ham	5 oz
150 g	emmenthal cheese	5 oz
1 tbs	prepared mustard	1 tbs
1	knob butter	1
	salt	
	nutmeg	

Pour the prepared meat stock into a pan. Add the lemon juice, nutmeg and a pinch of salt. Bring to the boil and add the cauliflower. Cover and cook over a gentle heat for the first 10–15 minutes. Then remove the lid and continue cooking for 5–10 minutes until the stock has almost evaporated. Drain the cauliflower in a colander and then put in a buttered fireproof dish. Spread the ham slices with mustard and lay on top of the cauliflower, mustard-side down. Cover the ham with the cheese cut into thin slices.
Place in a preheated moderate oven (180°C/350°F/Gas 4) and bake for 15–20 minutes until the cheese has melted and turned a lovely golden brown.
Serve immediately. This is a very simple dish to prepare and is both light and nourishing.

French-bean gulyás

400 g	beef stew (see p. 61)	1 lb
1 kg	French or runner beans	2¼ lb
1	clove garlic	1
100 ml	soured cream	4 fl oz
1	small bunch parsley	1
	salt	

Prepare the beef stew following the instructions on page 61 and cook until nearly all the liquid has evaporated. Clean the French beans and cut into 3–4 cm (1¼–1½ in) pieces. Place in a pan of lightly salted, boiling water. Add the whole garlic and cook over a moderate heat until the beans are tender. Discard the garlic. Drain the beans in a colander. (Do not throw away the bean water, it will make an excellent base for a soup.)
Add the soured cream to the beef and bring to the

boil. Mix in the French beans, stirring carefully to avoid breaking them. Cook for a few more minutes. Adjust seasoning with salt if necessary. Spoon carefully into a deep hot serving dish and sprinkle with a little finely chopped parsley. Serve at once.

Note! I usually prepare this dish when I have some stew left over. It is delicious and very sustaining and can be warmed up several times, but shake the pan rather than using a spoon, otherwise the beans will get broken.

Baked French beans

1 kg	French or runner beans (fresh, deep-frozen or canned)	2¼ lb
300 g	spicy soft sausage	11 oz
2	hard boiled eggs	2
200 ml	soured cream	7 fl oz
2 tbs	oil	2 tbs
80 g	hard grated cheese	3 oz
1	clove garlic	1
	salt	
	pepper	
	breadcrumbs	
1	knob butter	1

Place the prepared green beans in a pan of lightly salted boiling water. Add the whole garlic and cook until half done. Discard the garlic and drain the beans in a colander. Slice the sausage and mix with the beans. Butter a fireproof dish and sprinkle with breadcrumbs. Spoon the beans in the dish and arrange the sliced hard boiled eggs on top. Season with salt and pepper.

Blend the soured cream, oil and grated cheese thoroughly together. Add a little salt and pour

French-bean gulyás

over the beans. Cover with kitchen foil and bake for 15 minutes in a moderate oven (180° C/350° F/ Gas 4). Remove the foil, increase the temperature to 220° C/425° F/Gas 7 and continue baking for about 10 minutes until the top is a rich golden brown. Serve at once, for like every baked cheese and soured cream dish, it is only nice hot.

Hungarian-style green beans with curd cheese and dill

1 kg	runner or French beans (fresh or deep-frozen)	2 ¼ lb
100 g	cheddar, emmenthal or edam cheese	4 oz
150 g	soft ewe's milk curd cheese	5 oz
200 ml	soured cream	7 fl oz
40 g	butter	1 ½ oz
1	bunch fresh dill	1
1	clove garlic	1
	salt	
	breadcrumbs	
1	egg yolk	1

Ham, cheese and leek strudel

Wash and trim the green beans and cook over a gentle heat in slightly salted boiling water with the garlic until tender. Discard the garlic and drain the beans in a colander. Place in a bowl and while still hot add the coarsely grated cheese, the crumbled curd cheese and the finely chopped dill. Toss lightly together, taking care not to break the beans.

Butter a fireproof dish and dust with breadcrumbs. Spoon in the green beans, smoothing the top, then add the beaten egg yolk, the lightly salted soured cream and the chopped butter. Bake in a hot oven (220–230° C/425–450° F/Gas 7–8) for 10–15 minutes until the top is golden brown. Serve piping hot.

Ham, cheese and leek strudel

	for the pastry		
180 g	plain flour	6 oz
1	egg	1
1 tsp	oil	1 tsp
1 tsp	lemon juice	1 tsp
	salt	
1	egg yolk to brush the pastry	1
	for the filling	
6	medium sized leeks	6
200 g	cooked sliced ham	7 oz
2	eggs	2
150 g	grated cheddar cheese	5 oz
1	knob butter	1
	salt	
	pepper	
	caraway seed	
	nutmeg	

Put the flour into a bowl, add a pinch of salt, the beaten egg, the oil and enough tepid water to make a fairly soft, pliable pastry. Shape into a ball and put aside for 30 minutes.

Wash the leeks and remove the green tops. Cut into 4 pieces and cook in lightly salted boiling water over a moderate heat for 10–15 minutes until half-cooked. Drain in a colander and leave to cool. Beat the eggs together with the grated cheese and season to taste with salt and nutmeg.

Roll the pastry into a thin sausage shape on a floured tea towel. Cover with the sliced ham to within 4 cm (1¾ in) of the edges. Lay the leeks evenly on the ham and finally spread with the egg mixture. Lift the edge of the cloth and roll up the strudel fairly loosely. Dampen the edges with water and press gently together. Tuck the ends underneath to prevent the filling from coming out. Lay on a buttered baking tray, brush with beaten egg and sprinkle generously with caraway seeds. Bake in a moderate oven (180° C/350° F/Gas 4) for 30–35 minutes or until golden brown. Leave 5–10 minutes before serving.

Cheese-and-leek flan

	for the pastry	
200 g	plain flour	7 oz
100 g	butter or margarine	4 oz
100 g	cheese spread	4 oz
	salt	
	for the filling	
750 g	leeks	1¾ lb
30 g	flour	1 oz
50 g	butter	2 oz
150 ml	milk	¼ pt
100 ml	whipping cream	4 fl oz
80 g	grated cheese	3 oz
	nutmeg	
	salt	
	pepper	

Sift the flour and a pinch of salt into a bowl. Rub in the butter, blend with the cheese and 1–2 table-spoons of water to make a fairly soft pastry. Roll out on a floured surface and line a buttered and floured flan tin. Prick the bottom with a fork. Bake blind in a moderate oven (180° C/350° F/Gas 4) for 15 minutes.
Wash the leeks thoroughly and use only the white stems. Place in a pan of boiling, lightly salted water and cook until soft. Drain the leeks through a colander and reserve the water for later use.
Prepare a béchamel sauce (see p. 61) using the butter, flour, milk and 150 ml (5 fl oz) of the leek water. Leave to cool, then season with salt, pepper and nutmeg. Whip the cream and fold lightly into the sauce. Place the leeks on a kitchen towel or absorbent paper to soak up any moisture. Spread a layer of béchamel sauce in the flan case followed by a layer of leeks. Continue alternating between the sauce and the leeks, finishing with a layer of leeks. Sprinkle the top with grated cheese and bake in a moderate oven (180° C/350° F/Gas 4) for 30 minutes or until golden brown. Serve whilst still slightly warm.

Bacon-and-leek tart

400 g	deep frozen puff pastry	1 lb
8–10	young leeks	8–10
150 g	lean smoked bacon	5 oz
4	eggs	4
200–300 ml	soured cream	7–11 fl oz
2 level tsp	seasoning salt	2 level tsp
	nutmeg	
	salt	
	pepper	
	caraway seed	

Roll out the pastry on a floured surface to line the bottom and sides of a medium-sized rectangular baking tray. Prick the bottom with a fork.
Wash the leeks and use only the white parts. Cut into thin slices. Dice the bacon and fry. Remove the bacon with a perforated spoon and put aside. Add the sliced leeks to the pan and fry until trans-parent. Take out with a perforated spoon and leave to cool. Then place in a bowl and add the beaten eggs, soured cream, seasoning salt and the other flavourings to taste. Mix thoroughly to-gether.
Spread over the pastry, sprinkle with the bacon and bake in a moderate oven (180° C/350° F/Gas 4) for 25–30 minutes until golden brown.
Take out of the flan case and place on a chopping board or flat dish. Cut into wedges and serve hot.

Stuffed aubergine

4 (800 g)	aubergine	4 (1¾ lb)
4	hard boiled eggs	4
150 g	cooked ham	5 oz
150 g	salty ewe's milk cheese	5 oz
3 tbs	oil	3 tbs
1 tbs	breadcrumbs	1 tbs
1	knob butter	1
	salt	
	freshly ground white pepper	
300 ml	tomato sauce (see p. 61)	½ pt

Wash the aubergine, remove the stems and cut lengthwise. Rub salt onto the cut surfaces and put aside for 30 minutes. Rinse in running water and dry on absorbent paper. Pour the oil into a large baking tray and lay the aubergine halves cut side down in a row. Bake in a moderate oven (180° C/ 350° F/Gas 4) for 30 minutes.

Meanwhile, dice the ham, cheese and hard boiled eggs into a bowl. Season to taste with salt and sprinkle generously with white pepper. Mix lightly together. Turn the pre-baked aubergine halves over and spoon in the stuffing. Butter a fireproof dish and dust with breadcrumbs. Arrange the aubergine in the dish, sprinkle with the juice from the baking tray and return to a hot oven (200° C/ 400° F/Gas 4) for 15–20 minutes until the cheese has melted.

Serve at once, with the hot tomato sauce in a separate sauceboat.

Portuguese stuffed aubergine with popcorn

4	medium aubergines	4
500 ml	popcorn	1 pt
300 g	sardines in oil	11 oz
4–5	fresh mint or basil	4–5
2	hard boiled eggs	2
1	knob butter	1
1 tsp	prepared mustard	1 tsp
1	egg yolk	1
2 tbs	oil	2 tbs
	salt	

Wash the aubergines, slice them in half lengthwise and cut out the middle leaving approximately 2 cm (½ in) in thickness. Sprinkle with salt and put aside for 1 hour. Rinse in cold water and dry thoroughly on absorbent paper. Drain the flesh from the middle in a colander.

Put the popcorn into a deep dish, then add the sardines mashed into small pieces, the chopped mint, the flesh from the aubergine, the diced hard boiled eggs, the egg yolk, 1 tablespoon of oil (you could use the oil from the sardines) and mix together carefully.

Beat the mustard and butter together until smooth, spread onto the insides of the aubergine, then spoon in the stuffing.

Lay the aubergine in an oiled fireproof dish and bake in a moderate oven (180° C/350° F/Gas 4) for 35–40 minutes.

If the top browns too quickly, cover with kitchen foil or greaseproof paper. Do not shorten the baking time, otherwise the aubergine will not cook through. This dish is delicious served both hot or cold.

Portuguese stuffed aubergine with popcorn

Layered aubergine and courgette, Parma style

600 g	young aubergines	1¼ lb
600 g	young courgettes	1¼ lb
300 g	soft, moist cheese	11 oz
50 g	parmesan type cheese	2 oz
500 g	freshly made tomato sauce (see p. 61)	1 lb
1–2 tbs	oil	1–2 tbs
½ tsp	dried rosemary	½ tsp
½ tsp	dried thyme	½ tsp
	salt	
	pepper	
	a little flour	
	oil for deep frying	

Blanch the washed aubergine for 1–2 minutes in boiling water, remove the skin, then cut into thin slices lengthwise. Sprinkle with salt and put aside for 30 minutes. Rinse in running water and dry with absorbent paper. Turn in flour and fry in plenty of oil. Drain on absorbent paper. Wash the courgettes and repeat the same process as for the aubergine, but do not peel. Prepare the tomato sauce, grate the parmesan and cut the soft cheese into thin slices. Place a layer of aubergine in the bottom of an oiled fireproof dish. Sprinkle with salt and pepper, herbs, a little grated cheese and some slices of cheese. Then pour a few table-spoons of the tomato sauce on top. Add the next layer using the courgettes, herbs, cheese and tomato sauce. Continue alternating between the aubergine and courgettes until all the ingredients have been used up, finishing with cheese and tomato sauce. Sprinkle the top with oil and bake in a hot oven (200–220° C/400–425° F/Gas 6–7) for 25–30 minutes until golden brown.

Serve immediately with grated cheese.

Layered pepper, courgette and ham

(for 4–6 people)

1 kg	yellow, red and green peppers	2¼ lb
500 g	courgettes	1 lb
250 g	ham	½ lb
150 g	emmenthal cheese	5 oz
2	eggs	2

19

Courgettes stuffed with mushrooms

100 ml	single cream	4 fl oz
50 g	grated parmesan cheese	2 oz
	salt	
	pepper	
	nutmeg	
1	knob butter	1
	parsley	

Use only large fleshy peppers for this recipe. Wash and dry the peppers, place on a baking tray and bake for a few minutes in a hot oven (220° C/425° F/Gas 7), turning them over several times. Remove the baking tray from the oven and cover with kitchen foil for 5 minutes. The peppers will go very soft in the steam, enabling the skin to be peeled off with ease. Halve each pepper lengthwise, remove the core and carefully place in a colander to drain.

Line a buttered shallow cake tin approximately 20 cm (8 in) in diameter with the peppers, placing the pointed end in the middle and allowing 4 cm (1½ in) to extend over the edge of the tin. Arrange the slices of ham, cut into thirds or halves, in a starlike pattern on top, also extending over the edge of the tin. Wash and slice the courgettes, placing half of them on top of the ham, followed by all the cheese cut into thin slices, and then the rest of the courgettes.

Beat the eggs in a bowl with the cream, adding the grated cheese and a pinch of nutmeg. Season to taste with salt and pepper and pour over the courgettes. Fold the ham and pepper over the egg mixture and press gently. Stand in a baking tray containing hot water and bake in a moderate oven (180° C/350° F/Gas 4) for 50 minutes.

Remove from the oven and turn out on to a hot serving plate. Sprinkle with a little parsley and serve immediately cut into wedges.

Courgettes stuffed with mushrooms

4 (1 kg)	medium to large courgettes	4 (2¼ lb)
300 g	flat mushrooms	11 oz
1	small onion	1
1	bunch parsley	1
30 g	tomato purée	1 oz
1	clove garlic	1
300 g	spicy salami or sausage	11 oz
1 tbs	oil	1 tbs
	salt	
	pepper	

Wash the courgettes and slice in half lengthwise. Remove a few teaspoonfuls of flesh and place in a bowl. Add the washed and diced mushrooms. Fry the finely chopped onion in a pan with a little oil until transparent, then add the mushroom-and-courgette mixture and the crushed garlic. Season to taste with salt and pepper and add the tomato purée mixed with enough water to make a fairly thick sauce. Simmer for 10–15 minutes without a lid. Finally, add the diced salami and the chopped parsley. Mix well together, then fill the courgette halves. Arrange in an oiled fireproof dish and bake in a moderate oven (180° C/350° F/Gas 4) for 35–40 minutes.

It is delicious served hot or cold.

Stuffed marrow with tarragon

1 kg	vegetable marrow	2¼ lb
100 g	smoked streaky bacon	4 oz
400 g	minced pork of beef	1 lb
1	small onion	1
1	clove garlic	1
1	egg	1
100 g	mushrooms	4 oz
1	small bunch parsley	1

	salt	
	pepper	
8–10	fresh tarragon	8–10
200 ml	soured cream	7 fl oz
1	knob butter	1
	breadcrumbs	
2 tbs	grated cheese	2 tbs

Wash and peel the marrow and cut in half lengthwise. Remove the seeds and sprinkle with a little salt. Dice the bacon and fry. Add the finely chopped onion and cook until transparent. Then add the minced meat and the washed and finely sliced mushroom. Fry over a high heat for 4–5 minutes stirring frequently. Remove from the heat and when cool, stir in the beaten egg, the crushed garlic and the finely chopped parsley. Season to taste with salt and pepper and mix thoroughly. Dry the insides of the marrow and fill with the stuffing. Butter a fireproof dish and sprinkle with breadcrumbs. Place the stuffed marrow in the dish.

Beat the soured cream and grated cheese and chopped tarragon until smooth. Spoon over the marrow and bake in a moderate oven (180° C/350° F/ Gas 4) for 35–40 minutes until a rich golden brown. Serve hot or cold.

Note! This tasty dish can also be prepared with *courgettes*. Allow 2 fairly large courgettes per person.

Stuffed tomatoes, Genoese style

300 g	tuna fish (canned in brine or deep-frozen)	11 oz
200 g	rice	7 oz
4	large fleshy tomatoes	4
10–15	fresh basil leaves	10–15
30 g	blanched almonds	1 oz
1	large red pickled pepper	1
2 tbs	oil	2 tbs
2	egg yolks	2
	salt pepper	

Cut the drained fish into small cubes. Boil the rice in salted water until half cooked, then drain and rinse in cold water. Wash the tomatoes, cut in half and remove the seeds. Sprinkle with a little salt, turn upside down and put aside for 30 minutes. Meanwhile finely chop the basil and the almonds into a bowl and add 1 tablespoon of oil. Season to taste with salt and pepper, then mix together thoroughly. Spread the insides of the tomatoes with the almond mixture. Mix together the fish, rice,

the pickled pepper cut into thin strips, the egg yolks and a little freshly ground pepper. Stuff tomatoes with the mixture. Arrange the stuffed tomatoes in an oiled fireproof dish. Sprinkle with the remaining oil and bake in a moderate oven (180° C/350° F/Gas 4) for 35–40 minutes.

The tomatoes have a delicious piquant flavour and are excellent served hot or cold.

Semolina and meat cakes with tomato sauce

400 g	semolina	1 lb
200 g	minced cooked pork	7 oz
100 g	smoked minced pork flank	4 oz
100 g	butter	4 oz
1	egg	1
50 g	grated cheese	2 oz
1	clove garlic	1
	nutmeg	
	salt	
	pepper	
200 ml	tomato sauce (see p. 61)	7 fl oz

Semolina and meat cakes with tomato sauce

Gradually add the semolina to 500 ml (1 pt) of boiling salted water and cook over a high heat stirring all the time until done. While it is still hot, beat in the 80 g (3 oz) of the butter, the minced pork, the minced smoked pork flank, the crushed garlic and a pinch of nutmeg. Add salt and pepper to taste, and finally the beaten egg, stirring vigorously to prevent it from curdling. While still warm, tip out onto a wet wooden board or over-turned baking tray. Spread out until it is roughly 2 cm (¾ in) thick, then leave until it is quite cold. Using a 5 cm (2 in) pastry cutter, stamp out rounds. (Knead the trimmings together, roll out and make some more rounds.) Butter a fireproof dish using the remaining butter and arrange the rounds in circles slightly overlapping. Pour the tomato sauce on top, sprinkle with grated cheese and bake in a hot oven (200° C/425° F/Gas 7) for about 20 minutes, or until the cheese has turned golden brown. Remove from the oven and serve immediately.

Stuffed peppers

8	medium-sized, not very fleshy green peppers	8
1 l	tomato juice or	1¾ pt
100 g	tomato purée	4 oz
400 g	minced meat	1 lb
80 g	half-cooked rice	3 oz
1	small onion	1
1	egg	1
1	clove garlic	1
½ tsp	sweet paprika	½ tsp
	salt	
	pepper	
2 tbs	oil	2 tbs
30 g	flour	1 oz
1	celeriac leaf	1

Wash the peppers and remove the core and the veins. Fry the finely chopped onion in 1 teaspoon of oil, then leave to cool. Put the minced meat into a bowl and add the onion, rice, egg, crushed garlic and paprika. Season to taste with salt and pepper and mix well together. Stuff the peppers loosely as the rice will swell during cooking. (If there is any stuffing left over, shape it into small balls.) Pour the tomato juice or the purée diluted with 1 l (1¾ pt) water into a pan and bring to the boil. Add a little salt and the celeriac leaf. Put the stuffed peppers and the meat balls into the pan, cover with a lid and simmer for 30 minutes or until tender.

Meanwhile, prepare a roux with the oil and the flour. Add a little cold water and stir until smooth. Using a perforated spoon, lift out the peppers and meat balls, add the roux and cook for about 10 minutes, stirring until it thickens. Return the peppers to the pan and simmer for another 5 minutes. Serve immediately with a little soured cream. *Note!* Some prefer this dish on its own, but it is also delicious served with boiled potatoes.

Stuffed baked peppers

8	large fleshy peppers	8
500 g	cooked meat (any type)	1¼ lb
80 g	cooked rice	3 oz
1	medium onion	1
1	clove garlic	1
1	egg	1
1	small bunch parsley	1
50 g	grated cheese	2 oz
4–5	large tomatoes	4–5
100 g	smoked streaky bacon	4 oz
	salt	
	pepper	
	a little oil	

Wash the peppers, remove the core and veins and cut in half.
Mince the meat and fry the finely chopped onion in a little oil until transparent. Mix together in a bowl, then add the rice, crushed garlic, egg, chopped parsley and grated cheese. Season with salt and pepper and mix thoroughly together. Stuff the pepper halves, arrange them in an oiled fireproof dish and place 1–2 slices of tomato on top of each, followed by 1 thin slice of bacon. Bake in a hot oven (220° C/425° F/Gas 7) for a few minutes until the bacon is cooked. Serve immediately.

Argentinian sweet-corn and chicken salad

400 g	cooked chicken breast	1 lb
200 g	cooked ham in one piece	7 oz
300 g	cooked sweetcorn	11 oz
4	firm, fleshy tomatoes	4

Stuffed peppers

8	anchovies in oil	4
	mayonnaise made with 2 egg yolks (see p. 62)	
½ tsp	chili powder	½ tsp
2 tbs	ketchup	2 tbs
4	hard boiled eggs	4
10–15	olives	10–15
	juice and grated rind of ½ lemon	
100 ml	single cream	4 fl oz
	salt	
	parsley	

Bone the chicken and cut into thin strips and arrange in the bottom of a glass serving bowl. Sprinkle with the ham cut into small cubes, then cover with the sliced tomato. Season with salt, then add the drained sweetcorn and the chopped anchovies. Prepare the mayonnaise and beat together with the cream, lemon juice and grated rind until smooth. Add the chili powder and the ketchup. Season to taste with salt and pour over the salad. Chill for 5–6 hours.

Just before serving, decorate with the sliced or quartered hard boiled eggs, chopped parsley and olives. Accompany with slices of toast.

Bulgarian cheese and vegetable dish

2	tender, young aubergines	2
3	courgettes	3
1	green pepper	1
5–6	medium sized tomatoes	5–6
2	medium onions	2
2	cloves garlic	2
8–10	fresh basil leaves	8–10
2 tbs	oil	2 tbs
30 g	grated cheese	1 oz
100 g	salty ewe's milk cheese	4 oz
	salt	
	pepper	

Wash the aubergine and cut into thin slices approximately 1 cm (½ in) thick. Sprinkle with salt and put aside for 30 minutes. Rinse with cold water and drain in a colander. Wash and slice the courgettes. Cut the cored pepper and the peeled tomato into strips. Dice the onion, garlic and basil. Mix all the vegetables lightly together.

Oil a fireproof dish, spoon in the vegetables and

sprinkle the top with salt and pepper. Pour the oil on top and bake in a hot oven (200° C/400° F/Gas 6) for 30 minutes. Remove from the oven and lay the sliced or crumbled ewe's milk cheese on top, followed by the grated cheese. Return to the oven for a further 15 minutes.

Serve piping hot with fresh crisp bread and a light red wine.

Cauliflower, carrot and ham bake

2	medium onions	2
500 g	young carrots	1¼ lb
1	medium cauliflower (500 g, 1¼ lb cleaned)	1
250 g	cooked ham	½ lb
1	bunch parsley	1
500 ml	béchamel sauce (see p. 61)	1 pt
4	egg yolks	4
50 g	grated cheese	2 oz
	salt, pepper	
	nutmeg	
1 tbs	oil or butter	1 tbs

Cauliflower, carrot and ham bake

Bulgarian cheese and vegetable dish

shreds. Place in a pan with boiling water and a little salt and cook gently until done. Drain thoroughly in a colander.

Butter a deep fireproof dish, add half the cabbage and smooth the surface. Place the pork mixture evenly over the cabbage. Mix the tomato purée with 3 tablespoons of water and pour over the meat, followed by the grated cheese and the drained and diced olives and capers. Cover with the remaining cabbage, sprinkle with breadcrumbs and bake in a hot oven (200° C/400° F/ Gas 6) for 20–25 minutes. Serve garnished with chopped parsley and dill and slices of lemon. Warmed soured cream and some thin slices of rye bread with caraway seed are an excellent accompaniment.

Sauerkraut and haricot beans, Szerdahely style

200–250 g	large haricot or kidney beans	7–9 oz
600 g	shredded sauerkraut	1¼ lb
200 g	smoked flank pork	7 oz
1	bay leaf	1
1	quince or cooking apple	1
1	clove garlic	1
3 tbs	tomato juice or 30 g (1 oz) tomato purée diluted with 3 tbs water	3 tbs
1 tsp	slightly hot paprika	1 tsp
100 ml	soured cream	4 fl oz
1 tbs	plain flour	1 tbs
	salt	
	pepper	

Prepare the beans and meat in advance on the previous day.

Wash and place them in separate bowls of lukewarm water to soak overnight. Rinse the meat, place in a pan of boiling water and cook until tender. Lift the meat out of the pan and cook the rinsed beans, bay leaf and whole clove of garlic in the same liquid.

Simmer the sauerkraut in a little water, adding a little salt if it is sour. Remove the lid from the pan before the cabbage is completely tender and continue cooking until the liquid has nearly all evaporated. Put the beans in a large pan and mix with the sauerkraut. Add the peeled quince cut into wedges and the paprika. Bring to the boil and pour in the tomato juice. Blend the soured cream and flour together until smooth, then stir into the pan. Cook for a further 8–10 minutes and season with salt and freshly ground pepper. Finally, add the pieces of pork and serve.

Hot soured cream and fresh crisp bread complement the dish very well.

Note! This dish was originally cooked as part of the wine harvest festivities, but it is really delicious at any time of the year.

Transylvanian gulyás

500 g	lean pork *pörkölt* (see p. 61)	1¼ lb
1	clove garlic	1
1 tsp	caraway seed	1 tsp
800 g	sauerkraut	1¾ lb
1	bay leaf	1
200–250 ml	soured cream	7–9 fl oz
1	green or yellow pepper	1
1	tomato	1
	salt	

Prepare a *pörkölt* with the pork, adding the crushed garlic and the caraway seeds.

Rinse the sauerkraut in running water. If it is very sour, then simmer in a little salted water with the bay leaf until tender. If there is too much liquid, drain. Stir the soured cream into the *pörkölt* and bring to the boil. Add to the cabbage, stir gently and simmer for a further 10 minutes. Discard the bay leaf and decorate the top with slices of pepper and tomato. Serve piping hot.

Note! According to many Hungarian chefs, the cabbage and meat should be cooked together. But in my experience, it is better to prepare them separately, as the cabbage often tends to be overcooked.

Bavarian sauerkraut and liver dumplings

(for 4–6 people)

1 kg	sauerkraut	2¼ lb
2	medium onions	2
2	cooking apples	2
3 tbs	oil	3 tbs
500 ml	dry Riesling wine	1 pt
1	medium carrot	1
3	bay leaves	3
4	cloves	4
4	juniper berries	4
½ tsp	peppercorns	½ tsp

2 (400 g)	thick slices of pork	2 (1 lb)
4	frankfurters	4
2 (250 g)	liver sausages	2 (½ lb)
2 (250 g)	blood sausages	2 (½ lb)
200 ml	soured cream	7 fl oz
	for the liver dumplings	
200 g	pig's liver	7 oz
1	dry roll	1
1	egg	1
1 tsp	Season All	1 tsp
1	pinch nutmeg	1
½ tsp	dried marjoram	½ tsp
1	small bunch parsley	1
1	small onion	1
	salt	
500 ml	meat stock (made from a cube)	1 pt
	a little semolina	

To prepare the *liver dumplings*, soak the roll in lukewarm water. Mince the washed and drained liver into a bowl. Then add the squeezed roll, the finely chopped onion, the chopped parsley, egg, nutmeg, majoram and salt. Blend thoroughly together then put aside for 10 minutes. A little semolina can be added if the mixture is too soft or runny. Bring the meat stock to the boil and, using a dessertspoon to shape the dumplings, drop them into the pan a few at a time. Cook the dumplings for 5 minutes. Lift out and drain in a colander. Simmer the pork slices in the stock for 15 minutes. Remove from heat and lay the liver and blood sausages in the pan. Cover with a lid and leave for 10 minutes (but no longer, otherwise the skins will split). Lift out the meat and the sausages and drain.

To make the bed of cabbage, rinse in plenty of water (it should not be sour) and drain in a colander. Gently fry the finely chopped onion in 2 tablespoons of the oil in a large pan until transparent. Add the scraped and sliced carrot. Fry for

Transylvanian gulyás

33

a few more minutes, then add the cabbage and the peeled and sliced apples. Season with the bay leaf, cloves, juniper berries and pepper. Add a little salt, pour in the wine, cover with a lid and cook over a medium heat for approximately 1 hour or until tender. Finally, increase the heat and cook until the liquid has reduced.

While the cabbage is cooking, slash the frankfurters crosswise, brush with oil and grill on both sides for about 6 minutes.

Grease a large fireproof dish. Smooth in the cabbage, arrange the meat, frankfurters, sausages and liver dumplings evenly on top. Bake in a hot oven (200° C/400° F/Gas 6) for 15–20 minutes to brown the meat. Serve at once with hot soured cream and fresh crisp bread.

Note! This is an excellent dish for a cold winter's day, quite rich and sustaining, so it is not advisable for serving as an evening meal.

Transylvanian layered cabbage

1 kg	sauerkraut	2¼ lb
400 g	lean minced pork	1 lb
150 g	slightly hot paprika sausage	5 oz
50 g	smoked streaky bacon	2 oz
1	large onion	1
1	clove garlic	1
1 tsp	paprika	1 tsp
½ tsp	dried marjoram	½ tsp
100 g	cooked rice	4 oz
300 ml	soured cream	½ pt
	salt	
	pepper	
1 tbs	oil	1 tbs

If the cabbage is sour, rinse in running water and allow to drain. Then cook in very lightly salted boiling water until half done. Drain in a colander. Dice the bacon and fry in a large pan. Add the finely chopped onion and the crushed garlic. Cover and cook gently until the onion is transparent. Slice the sausage and brown slightly over a high heat. Remove the pan from the heat and stir in the paprika. Return to the heat and add the minced pork, a little salt, pepper to taste and finally, the marjoram. Mix well together and fry for 3–4 minutes over a high heat, stirring all the time. Cover the pan, reduce the heat to medium and cook for 25–30 minutes.

Grease a fairly shallow fireproof dish. Smooth a third of the cabbage in the bottom, followed by half the rice and half the meat. Add another third of the cabbage, half the soured cream, and the rest of the rice and meat. Finish with a layer of cabbage and the remaining soured cream. Cover with kitchen foil and bake in a medium oven (180° C/350° F/Gas 4) for 20–25 minutes. Remove the foil, increase the temperature to 200° C/400° F/Gas 6 for another 30 minutes or until the top is a rich golden brown. Serve piping hot.

A jug of soured cream should be set on the table as an accompaniment.

Variation: Instead of the minced meat and rice layers, 600 g (1¼ lb) liver sausage or a mixture of liver sausage and blood sausage can be used. Remove the skin and spread over the cabbage. Use the soured cream in the same way. The rice is not necessary, because there is rice or pearl barley in the sausages.

Bean and bacon dish

400 g	dried white beans	1 lb
200 g	lean smoked bacon	7 oz
1	bay leaf	1
1	clove garlic	1
1	small piece lemon rind	1
300 g	carrots	11 oz
300 g	potatoes	11 oz
½ tsp	dried thyme	½ tsp
2	stock cubes	2
2	slightly sour apples	2
	salt	
1	bunch parsley	1

Start preparing the bacon the day before you plan the meal. Wash and cook until tender in about 1 l (1¾ pt) water. Leave to cool in the liquid before lifting out to drain. Pick over the beans and soak them in water overnight.

Rinse the beans in cold water, then put them in the pan with the bacon liquid. Add the bay leaf, garlic and the lemon rind. Bring to the boil, then simmer until the beans are half cooked. Add the scraped and sliced carrots, the potatoes cut into cubes, the stock cubes and the thyme and continue cooking until the vegetables are tender.

Add the peeled and sliced apples and cook for another few minutes. Do not let them get too soft! Cut the cooked bacon into thin slices. Snip the bacon rind with scissors and fry for a few minutes. Spoon the vegetables into a deep, warmed serving dish, arrange the bacon on top and sprinkle with chopped parsley. Serve immediately.

Armenian beef and bean dish

200 g	dried mottled beans	7 oz
600 g	rump or topside of beef	1¼ lb
50 g	smoked streaky bacon	2 oz
1	small onion	1
2	cloves garlic	2
1	bay leaf	1
½ tsp	caraway seed	½ tsp
½ tsp	dried marjoram	½ tsp
1 tbs	tomato purée	1 tbs
500 ml	red wine	1 pt
300 g	mixed vegetables (carrots, turnips, celeriac)	11 oz
300 g	potatoes	11 oz

Pick over the beans and soak them in lukewarm water overnight. Then rinse them in cold water and leave to drain in a colander.

Fry the diced bacon in a large pan. Add the finely chopped onion and cook until transparent. Then add the beef cut into 2 cm (¾ in) cubes. Brown over a high heat for a few minutes before adding the crushed garlic, bay leaf, caraway seeds, marjoram and the tomato purée diluted with a little water. Pour in the wine and season to taste with salt and pepper. Bring to the boil.

Armenian beef and bean dish

Pour the beef ragout into the presoaked terracotta crock. Add the beans and enough water to cover. Cover with the lid and place in the cold oven. Turn the temperature to 200° C/400° F/Gas 6 and cook for 40 minutes. Remove the crock from the oven, remove the lid and add the prepared mixed vegetables and the potatoes cut into strips. If the liquid has evaporated add a little more water and return to the oven for another 30 minutes until the vegetables are cooked. The consistency should be fairly runny.

This dish is simple to prepare and very tasty.

Gulyás with beans

400 g	*pörkölt* made with beef (see p. 61)	1 lb
250 g	dried beans	½ lb
1	bay leaf	1
1	clove garlic	1
200 g	smoked meat (knuckle, pork flank, pork ribs, etc.)	7 oz
	parsley	

Start preparing the meal the day before you plan to serve it. Pick over the beans and soak them and the smoked pork separately in lukewarm water overnight.

Make the *pörkölt*. It is best to use a pressure cooker for this dish. Place the pork, the drained and rinsed beans, the bay leaf and garlic in the pressure cooker and cook until tender. Only add salt at the end, as the smoked pork will be quite salty anyway. Lift out the meat, bone it and cut it into small cubes.

Discard the bay leaf and garlic. Add the drained beans and the smoked pork to the beef *pörkölt*. Bring to the boil and add salt if necessary.

Serve sprinkled with chopped parsley and fresh bread.

Note! This is a very rich and sustaining meal. Soured cream flavoured with some finely chopped dill can also be served with it.

Bean and mutton bake

800 g	mutton (leg or shoulder)	1¾ lb
250 g	dried white beans	½ lb
600 g	French or runner beans (fresh or frozen)	1¼ lb

2	large onions	2
80 g	lean smoked bacon	3 oz
2	cloves garlic	2
300 g	potatoes	11 oz
2 l	meat stock (from a cube)	3¾ pt
½ tsp	dried marjoram	½ tsp
3 tbs	oil	3 tbs
	salt, pepper	
	Season All	
1	bunch parsley	1

Clean the beans and soak in water overnight. Remove any fat from the meat, cut into 3 cm (1¼ in) cubes and using a perforated spoon blanch in boiling water. Rinse in cold water and drain. Fry the diced bacon in its own fat and put aside. Heat the oil in a large pan. Brown the meat over a high heat for a few minutes then add the bacon, the finely chopped onion, the crushed garlic, the drained beans and the marjoram. Add seasoning salt and pepper to taste (salt is added right at the end). Pour in the meat stock, bring to the boil, cover with a lid and cook in a medium oven (180° C/ 350° F/Gas 4) for 1 hour.

Meanwhile, peel the potatoes and cut into cubes roughly the same size as the meat. Add the potatoes and the runner beans to the pan. Stir lightly, cover with a lid and return to the oven for another 30 minutes or until all the ingredients are cooked. Finally, season to taste with salt, add more pepper if necessary, sprinkle the top with chopped parsley and serve.

Note! Tarragon can be used instead of marjoram, but use only 1 or 2 pinches.

Dried peas and pork knuckle

400 g	dried peas	1 lb
600 g	lean smoked knuckle	1¼ lb
1	bay leaf	1
1 tsp	dried marjoram	1 tsp
1	large onion	1
1	leek	1
200 g	carrots	7 oz
1	consommé stock cube	1
	salt, pepper	

Wash the knuckle thoroughly and leave to soak overnight in lukewarm water. Pick over the peas and also put to soak overnight.

Rinse the knuckle and place in a pan with 1,5 l (3 pt) of cold water. Bring to the boil, cover and cook over a medium heat until tender. Lift out of the pan. Cut the meat off the bone, score the rind with a sharp knife, roll into a joint and secure with string. Put the rinsed peas into the knuckle stock. Add the bay leaf, marjoram and a little pepper. Cover with a lid and cook over a medium heat until half done. Meanwhile, clean and slice the onion and leek. Scrape the carrots and cut them into small strips. Add to the peas along with the stock cube and continue cooking until all the vegetables are tender. While the vegetables are cooking, bake the knuckle in a hot oven (200–220° C/ 400–425 °F/Gas 6–7) until golden brown and crisp. Then cut into slices. Arrange the peas in a warmed serving dish. Put the slices of knuckle on top and serve.

Ham dumplings with mixed vegetables

300 g	cooked ham	11 oz
1 kg	cauliflower	2¼ lb
400 g	carrots	1 lb
200 g	potatoes	7 oz
4	eggs	4
250 ml	milk	9 fl oz
100 g	grated cheese	4 oz
	seasoning salt, nutmeg	
	salt, pepper	
1	knob butter	1

Wash the cauliflower thoroughly and divide into florets. Place in a pan of slightly salted boiling water and cook until tender. Drain in a colander. Mince the meat. Add a pinch of salt and 1 egg. Blend well together. Using a tablespoon, shape the ham mixture into dumplings and cook in boiling salted water, a few at a time, for 3–4 minutes. Remove with a perforated spoon and drain well. Scrape the carrots and cut into finger-sized strips. Peel and thinly slice the potatoes. Put the potatoes and carrots in a pan with boiling, slightly salted water and cook for 5 minutes. Drain.

Butter a fireproof dish and arrange the carrots, cauliflower and potatoes in layers. Lay the ham dumplings on top. Beat the remaining 3 eggs lightly in a bowl, add a little seasoning salt and a pinch of nutmeg. Season to taste with salt and pepper, add the milk and the grated cheese, then pour over the dumplings. Bake in a hot oven (200° C/ 400° F/Gas 6) for about 40 minutes until the egg has solidified and is golden brown. Do not open the oven door for the first 20 minutes, otherwise the egg mixture will collapse like a soufflé. Serve piping hot.

POTATO DISHES

Potato paprika

1 kg	potatoes	2¹/₄ lb
100 g	smoked streaky bacon	4 oz
100 g	smoked spicy sausage	4 oz
1	large onion	1
1 tsp	paprika	1 tsp
1	yellow or green pepper	1
1	tomato	1
	salt	
400 g	German meat sausage or frankfurters	1 lb

Dice the bacon or cut it into thin strips. Fry in a large pan, then add the peeled and finely chopped onion. Cover with a lid and cook over gentle heat until the onion is transparent. Skin the smoked sausage (if this is difficult, hold under hot water for a few seconds first). Slice and fry with the onion for a few minutes. Remove the pan from the heat, stir in the paprika and add the peeled and chipped potatoes. Pour in just enough boiling water to cover. Season to taste with salt, cover with a lid and simmer. When the potatoes are half cooked, add the sliced pepper and the peeled and chopped tomato. Cover the pan again and simmer until the potatoes are done. Finally, add the skinned meat sausage or frankfurters. Bring to the boil and adjust the seasoning with salt if necessary. Serve at once with pickles or green salad.
Note! Avoid using floury potatoes. Serve in fairly deep plates, so that everyone gets some of the delicious sauce in which to mash the potato.

Stuffed potatoes

1 kg	large potatoes	2¹/₄ lb
300 g	minced pork	11 oz
1	egg	1
1	egg yolk	1
200 ml	soured cream	7 fl oz
1–2 tbs	oil	1–2 tbs
1	knob butter	1
1	small onion	1
1	clove garlic	1
¹/₂ tsp	paprika	¹/₂ tsp
1	small bunch parsley	1
	salt	
	pepper	

Wash the potatoes and cook them unpeeled in boiling salted water until half done. Peel while still hot. Leave to cool, then cut in half lengthwise and spoon out the centre.
Fry the finely chopped or grated onion in the oil in a large pan. Add the meat and brown over a high heat for a few minutes. Turn down the heat and simmer for 30 minutes. Leave to cool, then add the crushed garlic, the whole egg, the chopped parsley and paprika. Season to taste with pepper and salt. Mix well together then stuff into the potato halves. Spread the potato centres in the bottom of a buttered fireproof dish. Place the stuffed potatoes on top and bake in a moderate oven (180° C/350° F/Gas 4) for 20–25 minutes. Pour the soured cream into a bowl, add a little salt and mix with the egg yolk. Brush on the potatoes and bake for another 10–15 minutes until golden brown. Serve at once with fresh green salad or pickles.

Layered potato and egg dish

1 kg	potatoes	2¹/₄ lb
6	hard boiled eggs	6
100 g	smoked spicy sausage	4 oz
500 ml	soured cream	l pt
2	egg yolks	2

Stuffed potatoes

50 g	grated cheese	2 oz
100 g	lean, smoked bacon	4 oz
1	knob butter	1
	breadcrumbs	
	salt	

Wash the potatoes, cook them in their skins, then peel them while still hot and leave to cool. Meanwhile slice the hard boiled eggs and the sausage. Beat the egg yolks, soured cream and grated cheese together in a bowl and add a little salt.

Butter a fireproof dish and sprinkle it with breadcrumbs. Arrange a layer of potato slices in the bottom, followed by one of egg and sausage mixed together. Add a little salt and 3 or 4 dessertspoons of soured cream. Repeat the layers, finishing with a layer of potato and a topping of soured cream. Finally, cut the bacon into thin slices, snip the rind and arrange on top.

Bake in a hot oven (200° C/400° F/Gas 6) for 30–35 minutes or until the bacon is golden brown. Serve with pickles or a mixed green salad.

Note! The addition of the egg yolk to the soured cream stops it from being too runny.

Variation: Replace the sausage with *cooked ham* or *frankfurters*.

Layered potatoes with mushrooms

800 g	potatoes cooked in their skins	1³/₄ lb
400 g	mushrooms	1 lb
1	large onion	1
4	hard boiled eggs	4
1	egg yolk	1
300 ml	soured cream	¹/₂ pt
1	bunch parsley	1
	salt	
1	knob butter	1
1 tbs	oil	1 tbs

Fry the sliced mushrooms in the oil over a gentle heat for 5 minutes. Peel the potatoes while still hot and slice when cool. Slice the hard boiled eggs and the onion.

Butter a fireproof dish, place a layer of potatoes in the bottom, followed by a layer of egg and then onion and mushroom mixed. Sprinkle with a little salt. Continue to layer, finishing with potato. Beat the soured cream and egg yolk together. Add the chopped parsley and a pinch of salt. Pour over the potato. Bake in a hot oven (200–220° C/400–425° F/ Gas 6–7) for 25–30 minutes.

Serve immediately with a green salad or pickles.

French layered potato-bake

1 kg	potatoes	2¹/₄ lb
4	hard boiled eggs	4
3	eggs	3
400 ml	soured cream	14 fl oz
100 g	butter	4 oz
100 g	mild cheddar	4 oz
	salt	
	pepper	
	nutmeg	
	breadcrumbs	

Cook the potatoes in their skins and peel while still hot. Leave to cool, then slice. Slice the hard boiled eggs and grate the cheese.

Beat the 3 egg yolks with the butter until frothy. Stir in the soured cream and season with salt and pepper and a pinch of nutmeg. Fold in the stiffly beaten egg whites. Set 2–3 tablespoons of grated cheese aside. Put the potato and egg slices in a bowl with the soured cream mixture and the cheese and mix together carefully.

Butter a fireproof dish and sprinkle with breadcrumbs, then tip in the potato mixture. Shake the dish gently to get rid of any air spaces and sprinkle the top with the remaining grated cheese.

Bake in a hot oven (200° C/400° F/Gas 6) for 25–30 minutes until golden brown.

Serve at once with fresh green salad or pickles.

Layered potato-bake with cheese and tomato

1 kg	potatoes	2¹/₄ lb
600 g	firm, fleshy tomatoes	1¹/₄ lb
150 g	smoked, grated cheese	5 oz
50 g	emmenthal or cheddar cheese	2 oz
¹/₂ tsp	dried oregano	¹/₂ tsp
40 g	butter	1¹/₂ oz
1	bunch parsley	1
	salt	
	pepper	

Boil the potatoes till done. Drain and peel while still hot, then cut into slices. Also slice the washed and dried tomatoes.

Layered potatoes with mushrooms

Butter a fireproof dish. Place a layer of potato in the bottom, followed by a layer of tomatoes. Sprinkle with a little grated cheese, chopped parsley, oregano and melted butter. Continue the layers, finishing with the tomato. Cover with the emmenthal cheese, cut into thin strips.

Bake in a hot oven (200° C/400° F/Gas 6) for 20–25 minutes until the top is a lovely golden brown. Serve at once sprinkled with chopped parsley and a few olives.

Note! This dish can be enriched by the addition of a few slices of *cooked ham* or *meat sausage*.

Potato-omelette roll

	for the omelette	
100 g	cooked, mashed potato	4 oz
50 g	butter	2 oz
2	eggs	2
30 g	flour	1 oz
100 ml	milk	4 fl oz
50 g	grated cheese	2 oz
	salt	
	pepper	
	for the filling	
200 g	mushrooms	7 oz
3	eggs	3
100 ml	yogurt	4 fl oz
100 g	grated smoked cheese	4 oz
1	bunch parsley	1
	salt	
	pepper	
1	knob butter	1

For the omelette use a little of the butter to grease a baking tray approximately 20 cm × 30 cm (8 in × 12 in). Beat the remaining butter with the 2 egg yolks, the mashed potato, flour and grated cheese, putting 2–3 tablespoonfuls of the mixture aside. Season to taste with salt and pepper, then fold in the stiffly beaten egg whites. Spoon into the baking tray and bake in a moderate oven (180° C/ 350° F/Gas 4) for 10 minutes.

Meanwhile, *prepare the filling*. In a large pan, fry the very thinly sliced mushrooms in the butter for about 5 minutes. Beat the yogurt with the eggs and a little salt and pepper. Add this mixture and the chopped parsley to the mushrooms. When the baked omelette is ready, remove from the oven and spread the mushroom mixture evenly over the top. Roll up, sprinkle with the remaining grated cheese and return to the oven for 5–10 minutes, just long enough for the cheese to brown a little on top.

Serve sliced on a prewarmed oval dish, together with a fresh green salad and some slices of toast. This is a delicious dish, but it must be eaten straight out of the oven.

Potato-and-sausage bake

1 kg	potatoes	2¼ lb
150 g	German meat sausage	5 oz
120 g	dry spicy sausage	4½ oz
80 g	smoked ham	3 oz
100 g	lean cooked bacon	4 oz
1	egg	1
40 g	flour	1½ oz
	salt	
	pepper	
1	knob butter	1

Peel and wash the potatoes. Dry them well, then grate coarsely. Add the flour and mix well together.

Remove the skin from the meat sausage and the spicy sausage, and cut into thin slices. Dice the ham and bacon. Add the beaten egg, sausage, ham and bacon to the potato and mix well. Season to taste with salt and pepper. Spoon into a greased casserole dish and bake in a hot oven (200–220° C/ 400–425° F/Gas 6–7) for 45–60 minutes or until the top is golden brown. Serve piping hot with an onion salad or a mixed green salad with a lot of onion added.

Potato-cheese ring

	(for 6 people)	
1½ kg	floury potatoes	3½ lb
3	egg yolks	3
1	whole egg	1
	salt	
	pepper	
	nutmeg	
50 g	butter or margarine	2 oz
100 g	grated parmesan cheese	4 oz
250 g	German meat sausage	½ lb
3 tbs	oil	3 tbs
	breadcrumbs	
	a few lettuce leaves	
	parsley	
200 ml	soured cream	7 fl oz
2	cloves garlic	2

Peel and wash the potatoes. Cut into strips and cook in boiling salted water. Drain, then leave for 2–3 minutes in the covered pan. Mash while still hot, then add the egg, egg yolks, butter and cheese. Season with salt, pepper and nutmeg. Beat until frothy.

Skin the sausage and chop into small cubes. Flash fry in the oil for a moment or two.

Butter a ring tin and sprinkle with breadcrumbs. Smooth in half of the potato mixture. Sprinkle the fried sausage on top, then cover with the rest of the potato. Knock the bottom of the tin gently to get rid of any air. Bake in a moderate oven (180° C/350° F/Gas 4) for 45–50 minutes or until golden brown. Meanwhile, mix the soured cream with the crushed garlic and a little salt and chill. Remove the potatoes from the oven and put aside for a few minutes before turning out on to a round, prewarmed serving dish. Fill the centre with the lettuce leaves and sprinkle with chopped parsley. Serve at once cut into wedges.

Accompany with the chilled soured cream served in a jug.

Chicken liver and creamed potato cake

800 g	floury potatoes	1¾ lb
60 g	butter	2½ oz
100 ml	milk	4 fl oz
100 ml	soured cream	4 fl oz
2	eggs	2
80 g	grated cheese	3 oz
	salt	
	pepper	
	nutmeg	
	breadcrumbs	
400 g	chicken liver	14 oz
1	small onion	1
1 tbs	oil	1 tbs
½ tsp	dried marjoram	½ tsp
	pepper	

Potato-and-sausage bake

Peel and wash the potatoes. Cut into cubes and cook until soft in boiling salted water. Drain and mash while still hot. Add 50 g (2 oz) of the butter and enough milk to make them fluffy but not too soft. Leave to cool.

Fry the finely chopped onion gently in the oil until transparent, then add the washed, drained and diced chicken liver. Season to taste with pepper and sprinkle with marjoram. Fry over a high heat for 5–8 minutes, then season to taste with salt and leave to cool.

Pour the cream into a bowl and beat in the separated egg yolks, the grated cheese, a little pepper and a pinch of nutmeg. Mix with the mashed potato and the chicken livers. Finally, lightly fold in the stiffly beaten egg whites.

Butter a round cake tin and sprinkle with bread raspings. Smooth in the potato mixture and bake in a moderate oven (180° C/350° F/Gas 4) for 25–30 minutes or until golden brown.

Note! This dish is rather like a real soufflé, so only fill the tin two-thirds full and do not open the oven during baking. When it is done, remove from the oven and leave for a few minutes before turning it out onto a prewarmed serving plate.

Serve cut into wedges. Accompany with lettuce and pickles.

Potato cake with cheese

1 kg	potatoes	2¼ lb
750 ml	milk	1¼ pt
60 g	butter or margarine	2½ oz
2	eggs	2
1	egg yolk	1
1	small onion	1
80 g	grated cheese	3 oz
400 ml	béchamel sauce (see p. 61)	14 fl oz
1	pinch cinnamon	1
	salt	
	pepper	
	breadcrumbs	

Peel and wash the potatoes and cut into cubes. Simmer until tender in lightly salted boiling milk. Drain and mash. While the potatoes are cooking, fry the sliced onion in half the butter until transparent, then add to the potato. Make the béchamel sauce and mix it with the potato purée while still hot, then leave to cool. Beat the eggs and egg yolk together and add to the cold purée together with the grated cheese and cinnamon. Season to taste with salt and pepper and beat until fluffy.

Grease a baking tray or fireproof dish and dust with breadcrumbs. Spoon in the potato purée, smooth the top and sprinkle with more breadcrumbs. Melt the remaining butter and pour over the top. Bake in a hot oven (220° C/425° F/Gas 7) until crisp and golden brown.

Serve piping hot with a fresh green salad or some pickles.

Baked fish, old fisherman's style

1 kg	marine fish (such as tuna, cod, haddock)	2¼ lb
1	bay leaf	1
½	lemon	½
3 tbs	dry white wine	3 tbs
800 g	potatoes cooked in their skins	1¾ lb
5	eggs	5
300 ml	soured cream	½ pt
1	bunch chopped dill	1
100 g	grated cheese	4 oz
	salt	
1	knob butter	1

Wash and prepare the fish and lay in a large pan or baking tray. Pour over it enough lightly salted water to cover. Add the bay leaf, the sliced lemon and the wine. Bring to the boil, then simmer for 10 minutes. Carefully lift out the fish and drain on a rack.

Remove the skin and bones and put the fish in an oval buttered fireproof dish.

Cut the warm potatoes into cubes and mix with the beaten eggs. Beat the chopped dill into the soured cream, add to the potato, season to taste with salt and spread over the fish. Sprinkle the top with the grated cheese and bake in a moderate oven (180° C/350° F/Gas 4) for 30–35 minutes or until golden brown. Serve at once.

Potato dish, Lyon style

800 g	potatoes	1¾ lb
1	large onion	1
75 g	butter	3 oz

250 g	cooking spicy sausage	½ lb
200 g	chicken liver	7 oz
100 ml	meat stock (made with a cube)	4 fl oz
3 tbs	tomato purée	3 tbs
100 g	grated cheese	4 oz
500 ml	cream	1 pt
1	egg yolk	1
1	bunch parsley	1
	salt	
	pepper	

Cook the potatoes in their skins and peel while still hot. Slice fairly thinly when cool. Fry the finely chopped onion in 50 g (2 oz) of the butter in a large pan until transparent. Skin the sausage, crumble up and add to the onion together with the washed, drained and diced liver. Fry over a high heat for a few minutes. Stir the tomato purée into the hot meat stock and pour into the pan. Add a generous amount of pepper and cook over a high heat stirring frequently until it thickens.

Butter a fireproof dish with the remaining butter and arrange half the sliced potato in the bottom. Pour the thick ragout on top. Sprinkle with half the cheese, then cover with the remaining potato. Beat the cream and egg yolk together. Add the chopped parsley, season to taste with salt and pour over the potato. Sprinkle the top with the rest of the cheese. Bake in a hot oven (200° C/400° F/ Gas 6) for 45–50 minutes or until golden brown. Serve at once.

Potato cake supreme with tomatoes

for the pastry case		
250 g	flour	9 oz

Potato dish, Lyon style

150 g	butter or margarine	5 oz
2	egg yolks	2
2 tbs	madeira or sherry	2 tbs
	nutmeg	
	salt	
	for the filling	
750 g	potatoes	1¾ lb
2	large onions	2
4	large, firm, fleshy tomatoes	4
1	egg	1
200 ml	single cream	7 fl oz
1	clove garlic	1
1	bunch parsley	1
1	sprig rosemary (or ½ tsp dried rosemary)	1
150 g	parmesan cheese	5 oz
	salt	
	pepper	

Sift the flour into a bowl and rub in the butter. Add the egg yolks, madeira, salt and a pinch of nutmeg. Knead, shape into a ball, cover and place in the refrigerator for 1 hour.

Meanwhile, peel the potatoes and onions and cut into slices. Place in a pan with enough boiling salted water to cover. Cook for 10 minutes, drain and leave to cool. Wash and slice the tomatoes. Mix the cream with the crushed garlic, salt and pepper.

Lay the chilled pastry on a floured surface and roll out to fit a fluted flan tin. Grease the tin and dust with flour, then line with the pastry. Prick the bottom with a fork or cover the pastry with paper and weigh down with beans. Bake blind in a hot oven (200° C/400° F/Gas 7) for 20 minutes.

Remove from the oven and leave to cool. Lay on a baking tray. Sprinkle the bottom with one-third of the cheese, then spread half the potato and onion mixture over the cheese and sprinkle with a little of the chopped parsley. Add another third of the cheese, followed by the remaining potato. Finally, cover with the tomato slices, the rest of the parsley and cheese and the rosemary. Pour the cream sauce over the top and bake in a hot oven (200° C/400° F/Gas 6) for approximately 25 minutes or until golden brown. Remove from the tin and serve at once.

Note! If the pastry cracks during baking and the cream starts to come out, serve in the tin.

Layered meat loaf

	for the meat loaf	
600 g	minced beef or pork	1¼ lb
1	roll	1
100 ml	milk	4 fl oz
1	small grated onion	1
1	crushed clove garlic	1
½ tsp	red paprika	½ tsp
1	egg	1
½ tsp	prepared mustard	½ tsp
1	small bunch parsley	1
30 g	grated cheese	1 oz
	salt	
	pepper	
	breadcrumbs	
	for the layers	
500 g	potatoes cooked in their skins	1¼ lb
4	hard boiled eggs	4
2	medium-sized gherkins	2
400 ml	soured cream	14 fl oz
1	egg yolk	1
	salt	
1	knob butter	1

It would be best to prepare the meat loaf the day before, or at least some hours before you plan the meal, as it must be quite cold.

Soak the roll in the milk. Put the minced meat into a large bowl and add the well-squeezed roll, the onion, garlic, egg, mustard, chopped parsley and grated cheese. Blend thoroughly together. Season with salt and pepper to taste. Sprinkle an oblong cake tin or a deep fireproof dish with breadcrumbs. Using wet hands, shape the meat mixture into a loaf to fit the tin. Sprinkle the top with a few breadcrumbs and bake in a medium oven (180° C/350° F/Gas 4) for approximately 1 hour or until golden brown. Leave to get quite cold.

Butter a deep fireproof dish. Place a layer of peeled and sliced potatoes at the bottom. Sprinkle with a little salt, then add a layer of thinly sliced meat loaf, followed by a few slices of hard boiled egg and some slices of gherkin. In a bowl, beat the soured cream and egg yolk until smooth, add a little salt and pour some of the mixture over the gherkin. Smooth out the surface, then continue the layers until the ingredients are all used up, finishing with a layer of potato and soured cream. Bake in a hot oven (200° C/400° F/Gas 6) for 30 minutes, until it is a lovely golden brown on top. Serve at once with a fresh green salad and pickles.

Roast pork knuckle

4 (1–1½ kg)	medium sized pig's knuckles	4 (2¼–3½ lb)
1 kg	potatoes	2¼ lb
150 g	very small onions	5 oz
3 tbs	oil	3 tbs
1	bunch parsley	1
	salt	

Wash the knuckles carefully and singe off any hair. Drain in a colander, rub with a little salt and put aside for 30 minutes. Dry thoroughly with kitchen paper. Heat the oil in a large pan and fry the knuckles over a high heat on both sides. Add a little water, cover and cook over a medium heat until almost tender. Then transfer the knuckles and the liquid into a fireproof dish or meat tin. Add the peeled potatoes cut into strips and bake in a medium oven (180° C/350° F/Gas 4) until the meat is crisp and golden brown. Turn the potato over from time to time.

When the potato is half cooked, add the peeled and sliced onion.

Arrange the knuckles, potato and onion on a hot serving dish. Sprinkle the potato with chopped parsley and serve with a fresh green salad or pickles.

Note! This dish is really delicious only if it is eaten straight out of the oven. Although it takes a little time to prepare, the results are certainly worth it.

Bakony-style braised pork and potatoes

1 kg	potatoes	2¼ lb
400 g	boned leg of pork	1 lb
250 g	peas	½ lb
200 g	flat mushrooms	7 oz
2	cloves garlic	2
1	yellow or green pepper	1
1	tomato	1
	salt	
	pepper	
1	bunch parsley	1
	oil for frying	
	some lettuce leaves	

Wash the meat and cut into thin, finger-length strips. Heat the oil in a large pan and brown the meat over a high heat. Add the peas, the washed and sliced mushrooms, the cored and sliced pep-per, the peeled and chopped tomato and the crushed garlic. Season to taste with salt and pepper, cover and braise until tender. Remove the lid, turn up the heat and cook until the liquid has reduced.

Meanwhile, peel and wash the potatoes and cut into small cubes. Fry in plenty of oil, lift out and drain on absorbent paper. Stir into the meat at the last moment and serve piled onto a hot serving plate decorated with a few lettuce leaves.

Loin of pork or chicken with potatoes and vegetables

8	slices of pork loin or chicken	8
800 g	potatoes	1¾ lb
2	medium-sized carrots	2
100 g	runner or French beans	4 oz
100 g	button mushrooms	4 oz
1	small onion	1
	cloves garlic	

Roast pork knuckle

1	stick celery with leaves	1
1	small bunch parsley	1
1	green or yellow pepper	1
1	tomato	1
1	sprig rosemary	1
	salt	
	pepper	
	a little oil	

Boil the potatoes in their skins until half-cooked, and peel them while still hot. Leave to cool, then cut into thick rings or chips. Wash the carrots, green beans, mushrooms and celery and slice or cut as desired.

Wash and dry the meat. Rub with a little salt and put aside for 30 minutes. Dry on kitchen paper and fry on both sides in a little oil.

Soak the crock in water for 10–15 minutes, then lay the potatoes at the bottom. Arrange the meat on top, followed by the vegetables. Add the garlic, the parsley tied in a bunch, the rosemary, sliced onion, pepper and peeled tomato. Season to taste with salt and pepper. Finally, pour in the oil in which the meat fried, cover the crock with the lid and place in a cold oven. Turn the oven onto 200° C/400° F/Gas 6, and braise for 40 minutes after the desired temperature is reached. The vegetables will yield a lot of juice, so remove the lid at this point and cook for another 20–25 minutes for the liquid to evaporate. Serve at once.

Note! This is a deliciously light dish that can be prepared in advance and cooked later.

Pork with potato in tomato and pepper sauce (*lecsó*)

8	slices of pork loin	8
600 g	potatoes	1¼ lb
500 g	green or yellow peppers	1 lb

Pork with potato in tomato and pepper sauce (lecsó)

250 g	tomatoes	½ lb
1	medium onion	1
50 g	smoked fat bacon	2 oz
1	clove garlic	1
	salt	
	pepper	
½ tsp	slightly hot paprika	½ tsp
	flour	
	oil for frying	

Wash the meat, rub with salt and put aside for 30 minutes. Dry on kitchen paper, dip in flour and fry on both sides in a little hot oil. Drain on kitchen paper and put aside.

Wash the potatoes and cook them in their skins in boiling, lightly salted water. Peel them while still hot and cut into slices when cool.

Dice the bacon and fry in a large pan. Add the peeled and thinly sliced onion and fry until transparent. Sprinkle with the paprika, add the peeled sliced tomato and simmer for a few minutes without a lid before adding the washed, cored and sliced pepper and the crushed garlic. Season to taste with salt and pepper. Cover and cook over a medium heat until the peppers are half done.

Brush a fireproof dish with oil, lay the potato in the bottom. Sprinkle with a little salt, then arrange the pork slices on top. Smooth the tomato and pepper mixture – *lecsó* – over the meat.

Bake in a medium oven (180° C/350° F/Gas 4) for 15–20 minutes just until it has been heated right through. Serve at once.

Note! This is a traditional Hungarian dish and is very delicious. The potato tastes particularly good, as it has soaked up all the lovely flavours. It is an excellent dish for guests, as it can all be prepared in advance and just popped in the oven for 15 minutes before serving.

RICE DISHES

Rice and green beans

800 g	runner or French beans (fresh or frozen)	1¾
200 g	rice	7 oz
500 ml	meat stock (made with a cube)	1 pt
150 g	grated cheese	5 oz
1	bunch parsley	1
200 ml	ketchup	7 fl oz
	salt	
30 g	butter	1 oz

Wash the rice, drain thoroughly and fry in a large pan for a few minutes in the hot butter. Add the green beans sliced into approximately 3 cm (1¼ in) pieces. Pour in the hot meat stock, then transfer to a fireproof dish. Cover with a lid and braise in a hot oven (200° C/400° F/Gas 6) until the rice and green beans are tender.

Remove from the oven and stir in the grated cheese and the finely chopped parsley. Moisten a ring mould and spoon in the mixture, banging the bottom of the mould lightly to get rid of any air space. Leave in the mould for a few minutes, then turn onto a hot serving plate. Pour the hot ketchup over the top and decorate with a few sprigs of parsley.

Serve at once with a fresh green salad.

Rice-and-courgette bake

150 g	butter	5 oz
3 tbs	oil	3 tbs
2	medium onions	2
8–10	basil leaves	8–10
500 g	peeled tomato	1¼ lb
150 g	smoked streaky bacon	5 oz
600 g	young courgettes	1¼ lb
200 ml	meat stock (made with a cube)	7 fl oz
350 g	rice	¾ lb
50 g	parmesan cheese	2 oz
100 g	mushrooms	4 oz
	salt	
	pepper	

First, *prepare the sauce*. Peel and finely chop one of the onions, then fry until transparent in 30 g (1 oz) of the butter and the oil. Add the chopped basil and the mashed tomatoes. Season to taste with salt and pepper, cover with a lid and cook over a medium heat for 30 minutes.

Fry the diced bacon in 20 g (½ oz) of the butter. Fry the other finely chopped onion until transparent, then add the washed and sliced courgette and toss over a high heat for a few minutes. Reduce the heat to medium, season to taste with salt and pepper, add the meat stock, cover with a lid and cook for 20 minutes. Meanwhile, cook the rice in salted water until tender, then rinse and drain thoroughly. Stir in the sauce 50 g (2 oz) of the butter, and the grated cheese.

Grease a fireproof dish, place a layer of rice at the bottom followed by a layer of courgette and a few washed and finely sliced mushrooms. Continue with the layers until all the ingredients have been used up. Finish with a layer of rice. Dot with the remaining butter and bake in a hot oven (200° C/400° F/Gas 6) for 15–20 minutes. Serve at once.

Rice with courgettes, pepper and tomato (lecsó)

500 g	courgettes	1¼ lb
500 g	green or yellow peppers	1¼ lb
250 g	tomatoes	½ lb
1	large onion	1
100 g	smoked streaky bacon	4 oz
100 g	smoked spicy sausage	4 oz
200 g	rice	7 oz
1 tsp	red paprika	1 tsp
1	clove garlic	1
	salt	
	pepper	
	parsley	

Dice the bacon and fry in a large pan. Add the peeled and sliced onion and cook until transparent. Stir in the paprika and add the sliced sausage and peeled tomatoes cut into segments. Cook over a high heat until the juice from the tomatoes comes out. Then add the washed and peeled courgettes cut into small cubes, the cored and sliced peppers and the crushed garlic. Season

Rice and green beans

to taste with salt and pepper, cover and cook over a medium heat until half-done.

Wash the rice, stir into the courgette and *lecsó* mixture and cook until tender, stirring frequently. Add a little boiling water if necessary. Adjust the seasoning with salt and pepper, spoon into a hot serving dish, sprinkle with chopped parsley and serve at once.

Note! For a more substantial meal, sliced frankfurters or German meat sausage can be added to this dish.

Rice-and-meat, Bácska style

500 g	*pörkölt* made with pork (see p. 61)	1¼ lb
300 g	green or yellow peppers	11 oz
150 g	tomatoes	5 oz
200 g	rice	7 oz
1	small bunch parsley	1
	salt	

Prepare the *pörkölt* following the instructions on page 61, but cut the meat into smaller pieces.

When the meat is almost tender, add the washed and drained rice, the cored and chopped pepper and the tomatoes peeled and cut into wedges. Stir together, then pour on enough boiling water to cover by about 3 cm (1¼ in). Transfer into a fireproof casserole, bring to the boil, cover and bake in a hot oven (200–220° C/400–425° F/Gas 6–7) until the rice is done.

Garnish the top with some slices of pepper, tomato and some chopped parsley. Serve piping hot.

Ham-and-rice flan

300 g	long-grain rice	11 oz
1 l	milk	1¾ pt
	salt, pepper	
	nutmeg	
300 g	cooked ham or smoked pork flank	11 oz
100 g	ewe's milk curd cheese	4 oz
50 g	butter	2 oz
1	bunch parsley	1
400 g	deep frozen puff pastry	1 lb
1–2 tbs	breadcrumbs	1–2 tbs

1	egg yolk	1
	flour	

Cook the rice in the boiling milk over a medium heat with a little salt and pepper and a pinch of nutmeg, stirring constantly until tender. Stir in the butter and the curd cheese while still hot. Put aside to cool, then add the ham cut into thin strips and the finely chopped parsley.

Butter a round cake tin and dust with flour. Lay the thawed pastry on a floured surface and roll out thin enough to line the tin with overlapping edges 3 cm (1¼ in) wide and to cover the top. Sprinkle the pastry lining with breadcrumbs and spoon in the cold rice mixture. Smooth the top and lay the small circle on top. Fold over the edges and press gently. Brush the top with the beaten egg yolk and prick the pastry in a few places with a fork. Bake in a hot oven (200° C/400° F/Gas 6) for 25–30 minutes until golden brown. Remove the cake tin and slip the flan onto a hot serving plate.

Serve cut into wedges with fresh green salad.

Note! This dish is also very tasty when served cold.

Gourmet's veal and rice

400 g	lean meat (veal or poultry)	1 lb
1	medium onion	1
2 tbs	oil	2 tbs
1	bay leaf	1
1	clove garlic	1
1	small gherkin	1
100 ml	dry white wine	4 fl oz
½ tsp	hot paprika	½ tsp
250 g	long-grain rice	½ lb
500 ml	meat stock (made with a cube)	1 pt
1	bunch parsley	1
4	hard boiled eggs	4
1–2	tomatoes	1–2
	salt	
	pepper	

Wash and drain the meat, then cut into small cubes. Fry the grated onion in the oil in a large pan until transparent, then add the meat and brown over a high heat for a few minutes. Pour in the wine and add the bay leaf, the crushed garlic and the diced gherkin. Season to taste with the paprika, salt and pepper. (This dish should be fairly spicy.) When the wine has reduced by half, cover the pan and simmer until the meat is tender. Discard the bay leaf at the end.

Meanwhile, wash the rice and place in a fireproof dish. Pour in the meat stock, cover with a lid and cook in a medium oven (180° C/350° F/Gas 4) until tender. Remove the dish from the oven, and gently mix in the chopped parsley and the meat with the juices. Garnish the top with hard boiled eggs and tomatoes cut into wedges.

Serve immediately with a bowl of grated cheese.

Gyuvecs— a Serbian recipe

600 g	*pörkölt* made with pork (see p. 61)	1¼ lb
200 g	long-grain rice	7 oz
300 g	green or yellow pepper	11 oz
300 g	tomatoes	11 oz
300 g	aubergine	11 oz
300 ml	soured cream	11 fl oz
30 g	butter	1 oz
	salt	

Prepare the *pörkölt* following the instructions on page 61, then leave to cool. Cook the rice in boiling salted water, rinse and drain thoroughly in a colander. Wash and core the pepper, peel the tomatoes, prepare the aubergine (see p. 62) and cut them all into slices.

Gyuvecs—a Serbian recipe

Saffron-rice and chicken

Spread a layer of rice in the bottom of a buttered fireproof dish, place some of the pepper, tomato and aubergine slices on top and then a few spoonfuls of the *pörkölt* with its juice. Top with some of the soured cream and then repeat the layers. Finish with a layer of tomato and then soured cream. Dot the top with the remaining butter and bake in a hot oven (220° C/425° F/Gas 7) until the vegetables are soft. Serve at once.

Note! The addition of 1 medium sliced onion and 150–200 g (5–7 oz) of cooked green beans will make the dish even more sustaining.

Saffron-rice and chicken

1 kg	chicken breast or leg	2¼ lb
300 g	rice	11 oz
1	medium-sized carrot	1
50 g	celeriac	2 oz
2	medium onions	2
1	tomato	1
500 g	peas	1¼ lb
3 tbs	oil	3 tbs
2	cloves garlic	2
1 tsp	saffron	1 tsp
½ tsp	dried marjoram	½ tsp
½ tsp	dried thyme	½ tsp
	salt	
100 g	prawns	4 oz
100 g	canned mussels in oil (last 2 ingredients are optional)	4 oz

As far as the ingredients are concerned, this is quite similar to the famous Spanish dish *paella*. The method of preparation, however, is different. Wash the chicken and lay in a pan of 1,5 l

(3¾ pt) of water. Bring to the boil. Add a little salt, the peeled carrot, the celeriac, 1 onion and the tomato. Simmer for 30 minutes.

Meanwhile, cook the peas in a little salted water until tender.

When the chicken is done, lift out of the pan, remove the skin and bone and cut into small pieces. Strain the soup and put aside. Heat the oil in a large pan, fry the finely chopped onion over medium heat until transparent, then add the washed and drained rice. Toss in the oil, add the saffron and ¾ of the soup. Stir well, spoon into a fireproof dish, cover with a lid and cook in a hot oven (200° C/400° F/Gas 6) for 20–25 minutes until tender. Remove from the oven. Pour in the remaining soup, the braised peas, the drained prawns and mussels, the marjoram and thyme and the chicken. Then return to the oven for 5 minutes. Serve straight out of the oven.

Note! This dish can be prepared with *green beans* instead of peas. If *fresh herbs* are used rather than dried ones, the aroma will be even more enhanced.

Banana and coconut rice with turkey

500 g	boned turkey breast	1¼ lb
2	medium onions	2
2	apples	2
1 tsp	seasoning salt	1 tsp
1 tbs	dessicated coconut	1 tbs
1	bay leaf	1
2	egg yolks	2
100 ml	yogurt	4 fl oz
200 ml	single cream	7 fl oz
2 tbs	corn or rice flour	2 tbs
2	bananas	2
50 g	butter or margarine	2 oz
1 tbs	curry powder	1 tbs
150 g	rice	5 oz
300 ml	chicken stock (made with a cube)	11 fl oz
	salt	
	parsley	

Wash the meat and cut into 2 cm (¾ in) cubes. Peel and dice the onion and fry in 1 tablespoon of butter in a large pan until transparent. Then add the turkey, the pealed and cubed apple, the dessicated coconut, the bay leaf, the seasoning salt, a little salt and 2 tablespoons of water. Cover with a lid and braise over a medium heat until tender. If the liquid evaporates, add a little boiling water.

Meanwhile, wash the rice, place in a fireproof dish and pour in the hot chicken stock. Dot with a little butter, cover with a lid and bake in a medium oven (180° C/350° F/Gas 4) for approximately 20 minutes or until soft.

Beat the yogurt and eggs together in a bowl. When the turkey is tender, beat the cornflour with the cream until smooth and pour over the meat. Bring to the boil, remove from the heat and quickly stir in the yogurt and egg mixture. Remove the bay leaf, adjust the seasoning with salt if necessary and keep warm. Peel the bananas and cut in half or into quarters depending on the size, sprinkle with the curry powder and flash fry in butter on both sides for 4 minutes, taking care not to break the pieces when turning them over.

Smooth the rice on a hot serving dish and pile the turkey and banana on top. Sprinkle the top with a little chopped parsley and serve immediately.

Note! For those who are fond of unusual flavours, this dish is bound to be a special success.

Paella Valenciana

1–1½ kg	chicken	2¼–3 lb
2	large onions	2
2	cloves garlic	2
300 g	tomato	11 oz
300 g	peas	11 oz
400 g	rice	14 oz
1 l	chicken stock (made with a cube)	1¾ pt
100 g	shrimps	4 oz
100 g	mussels	4 oz
1 tsp	slightly hot paprika	1 tsp
1	bay leaf	1
1 tsp	saffron	1 tsp
4–5 tbs	olive oil	4–5 tbs
3 tbs	dry white wine	3 tbs
	salt	
	pepper	

Despite the number of ingredients, this dish is not difficult to prepare, it just takes a little patience and some inspiration. There are, however, some items that are essential for absolute success: a large, heavy but fairly shallow frying pan with metal handles, fresh shrimps or shellfish if possible, but if not, deep frozen or tinned will suffice. Wash and joint the chicken, rub with salt and put aside for 30 minutes. Peel and seed the tomatoes (see p. 62) and cut into segments. Peel and chop the onion and garlic, and if using canned shrimps and shellfish, drain them thoroughly.

Heat the oil in the frying pan, add the dried chicken, sprinkle with the paprika and fry over a high heat. Lift out and put on a plate. Fry the onion and garlic, pour in the wine and add the saffron. Boil for a few minutes, then add the tomato, peas, bay leaf and washed rice. Pour in the chicken stock, season to taste with salt and pepper and arrange the chicken pieces on top.

Cover the frying pan with kitchen foil and bake in a hot oven (200° C/400° F/Gas 6) for 20 minutes. Add the shrimps and mussels, cover again with the foil and bake for another 10–15 minutes or until the rice has absorbed all the juice. Serve straight from the oven in the pan.

Note! This is a traditional Spanish dish with almost as many variations as there are towns in Spain, but the delicious combination of flavours in this particular variation gives it the edge over the others.

Paella is traditionally cooked in the open over a wood fire or in a wood fired stove. This tends to lengthen the preparation time so that chefs in Spanish restaurants prefer to be told about the order one day in advance.

The secret of a really good *paella* depends on the variety of meat, shellfish and vegetables cooked in it.

Saffron is an indispensable ingredient in any *paella,* as it gives the rice that special flavour and a lovely golden colour.

The Castilians add anchovies, snails and green beans to their *paella.*

The Basque include carrots, parsnips and many fragrant herbs in theirs.

The Aragonians use a mixture of rabbit and pork instead of chicken. They also add green beans, artichokes and crayfish.

Provided you are willing to experiment, many delicious *paellas* can be made at home with a more limited variety of ingredients.

MISCELLANEOUS DISHES

Chicken and egg barley casserole, Orosháza style

1¼––1½ kg	chicken	2½–3 lb
2	large onions	2
3 tbs	oil or fat	3 tbs
1 tsp	slightly hot paprika	1 tsp
1	green or yellow pepper	1
1	tomato	1
200 g	egg barley *(tarhonya)*	7 oz
1	bunch parsley	1
	salt	

Fry the finely chopped onion in the oil in a large pan until transparent. Add the paprika and the washed and jointed chicken. Fry for 3–5 minutes over a high heat until the chicken turns white. Then add the washed, cored and sliced pepper, the peeled tomato cut into wedges and a little salt. Pour in a little water, cover with a lid and cook over medium heat until nearly done.

If most of the liquid has evaporated, add 100–200 ml (4–7 fl oz) of boiling water, stir in the egg barley lightly, cover and simmer, shaking the pan occasionally, for 10–15 minutes until the egg barley is cooked. The egg barley absorbs a lot of water, so add a little more boiling water when required.

Arrange in a hot serving dish, sprinkle with chopped parsley and serve at once with a jug of soured cream.

Fish soufflé

800 g	fish (cod, haddock – fresh or smoked)	1¾ lb
100–150 g	shellfish (in oil or brine)	4–5 oz
1	clove garlic	1
1	small onion	1
1	bay leaf	1
8–10	peppercorns	8–10
3 tbs	dry white wine	3 tbs
1	small bunch parsley	1
3	eggs	3

1	roll	1
100 ml	milk	4 fl oz
1	knob butter	1
2 tbs	oil	2 tbs
1	lemon	1
	olives	
	salt	
	pepper	
	breadcrumbs	

Prepare the fish (fresh water fish can be used as long as it is not full of bones), place it in a large meat tin or pan and pour in enough water to cover. Add the whole garlic, the sliced onion, the bay leaf, peppercorns, wine and a little salt. Bring to the boil, then simmer for 15 minutes. Remove from the heat and leave in the pan to cool. Soak the roll in the milk. When the fish is cold, lift it out, remove the skin and bones and mash in a large bowl. Add the squeezed roll, the egg yolks, salt and pepper to taste and mix thoroughly until smooth. Finally, lightly fold in the stiffly beaten egg whites. Butter a ring mould and dust with breadcrumbs. Spoon in the fish mixture and smooth the surface. Stand in lukewarm water in a deep baking tin and bake in a moderate oven (180° C/350° F/Gas 4) for 45–60 minutes. Do not open the oven, otherwise the soufflé will collapse! Heat the shellfish in the oil in a small pan, sprinkle with the chopped parsley and keep warm. Turn the fish soufflé out onto a hot serving dish, heap the shellfish in the centre and garnish with slices of lemon, a few olives and sprigs of parsley. Serve at once.

Onion-and-ham bake

400 g	cooked ham	1 lb
100 g	lean smoked bacon	4 oz
200 g	veal or loin of pork	7 oz

Onion-and-ham bake

2	eggs	2
2	rolls	2
2	medium onions	2
1	knob butter	1
100 ml	milk	4 fl oz
	salt	
	pepper	

Soak the rolls in the milk. Mince the washed and dried meat, the ham and bacon twice and place in a large bowl. Squeeze the rolls thoroughly and add to the meat together with the eggs, salt and pepper to taste. Blend well together.

Grease a fireproof dish, place one of the onions peeled and sliced on the bottom. Add the meat, smoothing the surface and top with the other onion, also sliced.

Bake in a moderate oven (180° C/350° F/Gas 4) for approximately 1 hour. Serve in the dish or turn out carefully onto a hot serving plate.

A mixed salad or pickled vegetables are an excellent accompaniment.

Gulyás in red wine

(for 6–8 people)

2 kg	chuck steak	4½ lb
100 g	oil or lard	4 oz
300 g	onion	11 oz
2 tsp	paprika	2 tsp
200 g	green or yellow pepper	7 oz
200 g	tomato	7 oz
1 kg	potatoes	2¼ lb
3–4	cloves garlic	3–4
1 tsp	caraway seeds	1 tsp
1	hot cherry pepper	1
200–300 ml	dry red wine	7–11 fl oz
	salt	

Traditionally, this dish should really be cooked over an open fire in a large cauldron or kettle with someone responsible for tending to the fire. However, it will be almost as good cooked in a large iron pot in the kitchen.

Wash and drain the beef and remove any fat or gristle. Cut into 3 cm (1¼ in) cubes. Peel and dice the onion. Heat the oil in a small pan and mix in the paprika. Pour a little of the oil into the iron pot, add a layer of beef, followed by a little onion, some slices of pepper and tomato, a little crushed garlic, a few caraway seeds, salt and then more oil and paprika, another layer of meat, etc. Sprinkle the top with the chopped cherry pepper. Cover with a lid and simmer over a medium heat for approximately 1½ hours, shaking the pot occasionally until the meat is almost tender. Then pour in the wine and add the potatoes, peeled and cut into large cubes or strips. Cover the pan again and cook until the potato is done. Nearly all the liquid will be absorbed by the potato. Serve in the pot, garnished with slices of hot pepper.

Layered egg, meat and mushroom casserole

8	hard boiled eggs	8
200 g	boiled or roast pork, or any other meat	7 oz
200 g	button mushrooms	7 oz
300 ml	béchamel sauce (see p. 61)	18 fl oz
1	bunch parsley	1
	nutmeg	
	salt	
	pepper	
1	knob butter	1
	breadcrumbs	

Peel the eggs and slice. Put the meat through a mincer (you can use up any leftover meat for this dish). Fry the diced mushrooms and the minced meat in half the butter over a high heat for 1 or 2 minutes, then put aside to cool. Prepare the béchamel sauce, leave to cool and then add a pinch of nutmeg, salt and pepper to taste and half the chopped parsley.

Butter a fireproof dish with the remaining butter and sprinkle with a few breadcrumbs. Place a layer of sliced egg on the bottom of the dish, followed by a layer of meat, mushroom and half the béchamel sauce. Then add a second layer of egg, meat, mushroom and béchamel sauce.

Bake in a moderate oven (180° C/350° F/Gas 4) for 30–35 minutes until the top is a lovely golden brown. Remove from the oven, sprinkle with the rest of the chopped parsley, and serve.

Serve this quick and easy dish with a mixed green salad.

Meat soufflé with egg

250 g	boiled or roast meat (pork, beef, veal, poultry)	½ lb

150 g	mortadella cheese	5 oz
50 g	grated ewe's milk cheese	2 oz
50 g	grated parmesan	2 oz
300 ml	béchamel sauce (see p. 61)	½ pt
1	bunch parsley	1
1	sprig rosemary	1
2	cloves garlic	2
2	whole eggs	2
4	egg yolks	4
	nutmeg	
	salt	
	pepper	
1	knob butter	1

Prepare the béchamel sauce following the instructions on p. 61. When cool, add a pinch of nutmeg and season to taste with salt and pepper.

Finely chop the parsley, rosemary and garlic. Mince the meat and mortadella into a deep bowl. Add the herbs and garlic, the cold béchamel sauce, the 2 eggs and the grated parmesan and ewe's milk cheese. Mix thoroughly together.

Butter a fireproof dish, spoon in the mixture. Smooth the surface, then with a small ladle, make 4 nests for the egg yolks.

Bake in a hot oven (220° C/425° F/Gas 7) for 45 minutes. Put an egg yolk into each nest and return to the oven for another 5 minutes.

Just before serving, sprinkle the top with salt and pepper and garnish with slices of tomato and sprigs of parsley. Serve piping hot.

Baked egg-and-tomato alla Napolitana

8	hard boiled eggs	8
1 tsp	anchovy paste	1 tsp
10–12	capers	10–12
1	bunch parsley	1
1 tsp	prepared mustard	1 tsp
500 g	peeled tomatoes (see p. 62)	1¼ lb
200 g	mushrooms	7 oz
1	clove garlic	1
6–8	fresh basil leaves or ½ tsp dried basil	6–8
8–10	olives	8–10
2 tbs	oil	2 tbs

Gulyás in red wine

Baked egg-and-tomato alla Napolitana

	salt	
	pepper	

Peel the eggs and slice in half lengthwise. Lift out the egg yolks and beat until smooth with the anchovy paste, the crushed capers, the mustard and half the chopped parsley, then spoon back into the egg whites. Fry the sliced mushrooms in the oil, then add the tomatoes cut into strips, the crushed garlic, the chopped basil and the olives. Season to taste with salt and pepper and simmer without a lid for about 20 minutes, until it resembles a thick sauce.

Spread 1–2 tablespoonfuls of the sauce in the bottom of a fireproof dish, lay the egg halves cut side down on the sauce and cover with the remaining sauce. Bake in a moderate oven (180° C/350° F/Gas 4) for approximately 10 minutes, just to heat the eggs right through. Sprinkle the top with the remaining chopped parsley and serve at once.

Note! Some grated parmesan cheese can be served separately.

Cheese flan with caraway seeds

for the pastry		
300 g	flour	11 oz

Cheese flan with caraway seeds

200 g	butter	7 oz
5–6 tbs	water	5–6 tbs
1	pinch salt	1
	for the filling	
150 g	emmenthal or cheddar cheese	5 oz
150 g	smoked cheese	5 oz
½ tsp	ground caraway seeds	½ tsp
3	eggs	3
200 ml	single cream	7 fl oz
	salt	
	pepper	
1	knob butter	1

Sift the flour and salt into a bowl. Rub in the butter, then add the water to give a fairly pliable pastry. Shape into a ball, cover and chill in the refrigerator for 1 hour.
Use a little of the butter to grease a round cake tin then dust with flour. Roll out the pastry fairly thin and line the tin with it. Prick the bottom with a fork and brush with the remaining melted butter. Grate the two types of cheese into a bowl. Add the egg yolks, the cream and the ground caraway seeds. Season to taste with salt and pepper and fold in the stiffly beaten egg whites. Pour into the pastry case and bake in a moderate oven (180° C/ 350° F/Gas 4) for about 40 minutes or until golden brown. Do not open the oven door for the first 30

minutes, otherwise the cheese mixture will collapse!
Remove from the oven, put aside for 5 minutes, then slip out of the tin onto a serving plate.
Serve hot or cold, cut into wedges, with a fresh green salad.

Ham-and-cheese soufflé

200 g	mixed hard cheese	7 oz
200 g	cooked ham	7 oz
4	eggs	4
400 ml	béchamel sauce (see p. 61)	14 fl oz
3 tbs	brandy	3 tbs
	butter	
	breadcrumbs	
	salt	
	pepper	

Grate the cheese coarsely and mince the ham 2 or 3 times. Prepare the béchamel sauce following the instructions on p. 61. Stir in the cheese while still hot (if it does not melt, heat the béchamel sauce up a little). Leave to cool, then beat in the egg yolks one at a time. Add the minced ham and the brandy. Season to taste with salt and pepper. When quite cold, lightly fold in the stiffly beaten egg whites.
Butter a cake tin and sprinkle with breadcrumbs. Spoon in the mixture and bake in a moderate oven (180° C/350° F/Gas 4) for approximately 30 minutes. Do not open the oven door for the first 20 minutes, otherwise the soufflé will flop! Turn onto a warmed serving plate and serve at once with lots of fresh salad.
Note! This dish is light, delicious and very quick to prepare.

Fondue with a difference (Raclette)

600 g	fat cheese that will melt easily (gruyère, emmenthal, edam, cheddar)	1¼ lb
1 kg	potatoes	2¼ lb
½ tsp	caraway seeds	½ tsp
	salt	
	pepper	

	pickled onions	
	small gherkins	

For this dish, you will need special individual fireproof earthenware dishes with handles or Caquelon and long fondue forks. It is wonderful as an "ice-breaker" for any party or for a lovely evening with good friends who have come to enjoy a really informal meal in good company. A little imagination can transform this extremely modest meal into something really special.

Wash the potatoes thoroughly, then cook them in their skins in plenty of boiling salted water, to which the caraway seeds have been added. When soft, drain and lay in a basket on several layers of kitchen towel, cover carefully and keep warm.

Cut the cheese into thin slices. Drain the pickled onions and gherkins and arrange in small serving bowls.

At the table everyone spears a piece of cheese on their fork and places it into their own individual pans over the spirit stove. Sprinkle the cheese with freshly ground pepper. While the cheese cooks (2–3 minutes), cut a hot potato in half and sprinkle with salt. Then spread with the melted cheese and eat with a little gherkin and pickled onion. Repeat this process until all the ingredients have been used up.

Serve with a dry white wine.

Note! Fondue is rarely eaten in this simple way. It nearly always has other additions, for example:
- 1 egg, some diced cooked ham, grated cheese, salt, pepper and nutmeg;
- 1 slice cheese, 1 slice cooked ham, 1–2 wedges of peeled apple;
- 1 slice cheese, 1 slice of tomato, 1–2 rings of pepper and a pinch of paprika;
- 1 slice cheese, a few wedges of peeled pear and pepper;
- 1 thick rasher of bacon with the rind scored, 1 egg, some grated cheese, 1–2 walnut halves, salt and pepper. The variations are endless.

It is best to arrange any additional ingredients in separate small bowls with the eggs broken into small cups.

Always serve with pickles and salad and let everyone choose their own combination.

Note! Since hot cheese is fairly heavy, to avoid indigestion and a sleepless night, it is advisable to plan a meal like this for late afternoon or early evening.

Fondue Bourguignonne (Meat fondue)

800 g	fillet steak	1¾ lb
1	potato	1
500 ml	oil	1 pt
3–4	sauces	3–4

Like cheese fondue, fondue Bourguignonne is also eaten as a communal dish.

Wash and dry the beef, then cut into 2 cm (¾ in) cubes. Heat the oil in the earthenware casserole or chafing dish over the spirit stove set in the middle of the table. Keep the oil bubbling gently. Place a small, carefully washed and dried potato in the oil from splashing. Everyone spears a piece of meat with a long-handled fork and fries it in the oil for 1–3 minutes, or as long as desired, then lifts it out and dunks it into one of the sauces. Take care, as it will be very hot! Then another piece of beef is speared and the same process is repeated. And now, here are some *sauces*, of which at least 4 should be prepared.

Fondue Bourguignonne (Meat fondue)

Garlic mayonnaise

Crush 4 cloves of garlic into a bowl, add 2 egg yolks in just the same way as for an ordinary mayonnaise, add 100 ml (4 fl oz) of oil, drop by drop, beating constantly. Season to taste with salt and pepper and add a few drops of lemon juice.

Piquant sauce

Finely chop a medium sized gherkin, crush 6–8 capers with a fork and mash 1 anchovy (or use 1 tsp of anchovy paste). Mix thoroughly with approximately 100 ml (4 fl oz) of mayonnaise.

Maltese sauce

Beat 100 ml (4 fl oz) mayonnaise with 100 ml (4 fl oz) plain yogurt. Add the grated rind and strained juice of 1 orange and a little salt and pepper. Beat until smooth.

Horseradish sauce

Fry 2 tablespoonfuls of breadcrumbs in 40 g (1½ oz) of butter until lightly browned. Add 100 g (4 oz) freshly grated horseradish and ½ teaspoon of sugar. Mix well together, then add 3 tablespoons of meat broth made with a stock cube. Cook for a few minutes, then leave to cool. Place in the freezer for a short time before serving.

Onion-and-tomato sauce

Combine a small peeled and quartered onion, 2 cloves of garlic, 2 tablespoons of a good quality oil, 2 tablespoons of tomato purée, 1 tablespoon of ketchup, a few drops of Worcestershire sauce and salt and pepper to taste. Liquidize until smooth and creamy.
Note! Any piquant sauce is good with a meat fondue. Mustard, chopped gherkins and chopped apple can also be served. Always serve with a mixed green salad.
Red wine is an excellent accompaniment.

Chinese fondue

1 kg	mixed meat (chicken breast, chicken liver, lean pork, veal, etc.)	2¼ lb
1 l	meat broth (made with stock cubes)	1¾ pt
3–4	different sauces	3–4

In some ways, Chinese fondue is similar to Fondue Bourguignonne. The similarities are that it is also served with several different sauces, and that the meat must be lean and cut into cubes of the same size (2 cm–¾ in). The meat is speared onto long-handled forks in just the same way, but it is not fried in oil but cooked in the gently boiling meat broth.
Some more sauces:
Curry sauce
Fry a medium finely chopped onion in 2 tablespoons of oil until transparent. Add 100 ml (4 fl oz) of milk, a little at a time. Simmer for 10 minutes. Mix 1 tablespoon of flour with a little water until smooth, then add 1 teaspoon of curry powder. Stir into the milk-and-onion mixture, simmer for another 10 minutes, then leave to cool.
Chinese sauce
Heat 2 tablespoons of oil in a small pan, add 3 tablespoons soya sauce, 3 tablespoons water and 1 tablespoon dry sherry, simmer for 5 minutes, then leave to cool.
Sweet-and-sour soya
and ginger sauce
Mix thoroughly together 2 tablespoons water, 4 tablespoons soya sauce, 2 tablespoons wine vinegar, 1 tablespoon icing sugar, 1 tablespoon honey, a pinch of salt and ½ teaspoon ground ginger.
Note! Mustard or mayonnaise with tarragon can also be served with Chinese fondue.
In accordance with the traditions of a Chinese meal, jasmin or green tea is served. If you decide to have wine instead, it should be white.

APPENDIX

Pork or beef pörkölt (Hungarian "dry stew")

800 g	lean pork or beef	1³/₄ lb
200 g	onion	7 oz
2–3 tbs	oil or lard	2–3 tbs
1 tsp	paprika	1 tsp
1	tomato	1
1	green or yellow pepper	1

Wash and dry the meat, and cut it into 2–3 cm (³/₄–1 in) cubes. Simmer the diced onion in the oil in a large pan until soft. Remove the pan from the heat and stir in the paprika. Return to the stove, add the meat and fry over a high heat stirring constantly. Then cover with a lid, reduce the heat to medium, season to taste with salt and add the peeled and seeded tomato (see p. 62) and the cored and sliced pepper. Add a little water, but only if the liquid in the pan evaporates. By the time the meat is tender, the onion will have been cooked to a thick, almost creamy sauce.
Note! If the *pörkölt* is for a casserole or a soup, reduce the quantity accordingly. On the other hand, it is a sensible idea to make a large amount, like 2 kg (4½ lb). It won't take any longer to cook and can be divided into small quantities and put in the freezer for future use.

Tomato sauce I

1 kg	ripe tomatoes	2¼ lb
2–3	sticks of celery	2–3
1	bunch parsley	1
1	large onion	1
50 g	smoked fat bacon	2 oz
1	pinch sugar	1
	butter	
	oil	
	salt	
	pepper	
	fresh basil	

Finely chop the onion, celery, parsley and a few fresh basil leaves into a bowl and mix together. (Dried or ground basil can be used, but it will not be so aromatic.) Dice the bacon and fry until transparent in a little oil and a knob of butter. Add the onion and celery mixture and fry until golden brown. Peel and seed the tomatoes (see p. 62), cut into strips and add to the pan. Season to taste with salt and pepper and add a pinch of sugar to counter-balance the acidity of the tomatoes. Cover and cook over a medium heat, stirring frequently until it thickens to a purée.
Note! The sauce will keep for 1–2 weeks in the refrigerator if stored in a screw top jar or covered china container, so the quantity can be increased if desired. Small quantities can be kept in the freezer for up to a year, or it can be bottled and put away for the winter. It is certainly worth spending time on this sauce, as it is the basic sauce for numerous Italian dishes.

Tomato sauce II

1 kg	ripe tomatoes	2¼ lb
1	large onion	1
2–3	sticks of celery	2–3
1	bunch parsley	1
1–2	medium sized carrots	1–2
	basil	
	salt	
	pepper	

Wash and chop the tomatoes. Dice, mince or grate the onion, carrots, celery and herbs and put together in a pan with the tomatoes. Cover and simmer for 45 minutes, stirring frequently, then pass through a sieve. If the sauce is too thin, return it to the heat and cook until it thickens. The sauce can then be bottled or frozen as desired in the same way as for tomato sauce I.

Béchamel sauce

If you want to prepare a béchamel sauce of medium consistency, there is one golden rule. For every 100 ml (4 fl oz) of sauce, allow 100 ml (4 fl oz) of milk, 10 g (½ oz) of butter and 10 g (½ oz) of flour. So for example, to prepare 500 ml (1 pt) of béchamel sauce you will need:

500 ml	milk	1 pt
50 g	butter	2 oz
50 g	flour	2 oz
	salt	
	pepper	

Melt the butter in a pan and add the flour. Cook until the roux is light brown, then add the hot milk a little at a time, stirring constantly. Beat with a whisk until smooth. Simmer for 10–15 minutes until the desired consistency is reached. Add salt and pepper only at the end.

Note! Increase or decrease the amount of flour depending on whether you want a thicker or thinner sauce.

Variation:

For a slightly richer sauce, a mixture of milk and cream can be used instead of only milk, or it can be replaced by meat stock, fish stock or vegetable stock, depending on what it is to be used for.

Béchamel sauce is rarely used on its own as described above. Usually, other ingredients are added like eggs, cheese or herbs, but then it will be known by a different name.

Mayonnaise

For every 100 ml (4 fl oz) of mayonnaise use 1 egg yolk, 1 teaspoonful of lemon juice and 100 ml (4 fl oz) oil. You also need a little salt.

So to make 100 ml (4 fl oz) mayonnaise, break the egg yolk into a small basin. Add a pinch of salt and the lemon juice. Then add the oil drop by drop, beating vigorously between each addition. As the mayonnaise thickens and becomes shiny, the oil may be added in a thin stream. Continue beating until it is stiff and holds its own shape. A mayonnaise may curdle if the oil was cold, added too quickly, or if the egg was cold or stale. But there is no need to worry, because it can be saved by pouring off the oil that has separated, adding a fresh egg yolk, and starting the process again.

Mayonnaise is the basis for innumerable cold sauces. It is, therefore, a good idea to prepare a large quantity, as it will keep in a wide-necked screw top bottle or jar for 1–2 weeks in the refrigerator. It is not advisable to freeze mayonnaise, as the oil will separate.

Mayonnaise with hard-boiled egg

Prepare the mayonnaise in the same way as above, but use hard-boiled egg yolk. The great advantage is that it will keep longer than when made with raw egg yolk.

Tartare sauce

Prepare the mayonnaise in the usual way, but use 2–3 hard-boiled egg yolks. Then add a small grated onion, a bunch of finely chopped parsley and 2 diced gherkins. Season with salt and pepper and a little strong mustard. Mix well together.

Preparing and cooking asparagus

Cut the woody parts off the base of the stems. Scrape the white part of the stems downwards, using a sharp knife or a potato peeler to remove the skin. Tie in bundles and stand in a pan with the heads up. Cover and cook over a medium heat in lightly salted water with a lump of sugar added. Do not immerse completely, the asparagus heads should cook in the steam. Drain well.

A steamer or a small deep pan is best for cooking asparagus. Failing that, lay the asparagus on a metal sieve in a large pan. Add just enough water to cover the bottom of the sieve so that the asparagus can cook in the steam.

Preparing tomatoes

Wash the tomatoes, then blanch them in boiling water for a few minutes. Remove from the water and the skin will come off easily, almost in one piece.

Bits of curled up tomato skin are really not a nice sight in a dish, nor are the seeds. So after peeling, cut the tomatoes in half and press lightly to remove all the seeds. But take care not to lose any of the juice.

Cleaning mushrooms

Wash the mushrooms carefully under running water, gently rubbing away any particles of earth or sand. Cut off only what is absolutely necessary from the stalk. Do not peel, otherwise a lot of valuable nutrients will be lost. Mushrooms tend to go brown quite quickly when sliced, so sprinkle them with a few drops of lemon juice unless it will spoil the flavour of the finished dish, in which case slice them just before cooking.

Preparing aubergines

Always buy small aubergines, because the younger they are, the better the flavour. The skin should be shiny and firm to the touch.

Wash the aubergine, then remove the skin with a wooden or plastic knife. Slice according to the recipe, lay out on a wooden surface, sprinkle with a little salt and put aside for one hour so that the bitter juice will run out. (If this is not done, the finished dish will probably taste bitter.) Rinse in running water, drain well and use according to the recipe.

The same process should be carried out in recipes where the skin is removed by blanching the aubergine in boiling water or placing it in the oven.

Important advice on cooking soufflés

The mixture can be prepared in advance except for the addition of the stiffly beaten egg whites, which must be added at the last moment when the oven has reached the required temperature and the soufflé dish is prepared.

Always make sure that the oven is at the right temperature, which, however, can be increased slightly immediately after placing the soufflé in the oven to make up for any heat loss. Reduce again after a few minutes.

Do not open the oven door for the first 20 minutes! After removing the cooked soufflé from the oven, prick with a meat skewer in 2 or 3 places to allow the steam to escape. This will prevent the soufflé from sinking. It is also very important to serve the soufflé as quickly as possible after taking it out of the oven. If it is necessary to turn the soufflé out onto a serving dish, you can either put the soufflé aside for a few minutes, although there is a danger that it will sink, or stand it in lukewarm water for a few moments before turning out. This can only be done, however, if a metal soufflé dish has been used. A pyrex dish might crack.

If you do not feel very confident about making soufflés, use a straight-sided dish instead of a fluted one, as the former will be easier to turn out. The safest of all, however, is the non-stick dish.

Home measurements

1 level tablespoon	
water, fruit juice, milk, soured cream, cream, brandy, liqueur, mustard, tomato purée	15 g – ½ oz
icing sugar	15 g – ½ oz
flour, castor sugar, curd cheese	12 g – ¼ oz
fat (butter, margarine, lard)	20 g – ¾ oz

1 heaped tablespoon	
flour, sugar, curd cheese	20 g – ¾ oz
1 knob fat	20 g – ¾ oz
a small glass of alcohol (rum, brandy etc.)	50 ml – 2 fl oz

Onion	
1 small onion	20 g – ¾ oz
1 medium onion	50 g – 2 oz
1 large onion	100 g – 4 oz

CONTENTS